Democracies to Come

Cultural Studies/Pedagogy/Activism

Series Editors
Rachel Riedner, The George Washington University
Randi Kristensen, The George Washington University
Kevin Mahoney, Kutztown University

Advisory Board
Paul Apostolidis, Whitman College; Byron Hawk, George Mason University; Susan Jarratt, University of California, Irvine; Robert McRuer, The George Washington University; Dan Moshenberg, The George Washington University; Pegeen Reichert Powell, Columbia College; Dan Smith, University of South Carolina; Susan Wells, Temple University

The Lexington Press book series Cultural Studies/Pedagogy/Activism offers books that engage questions in contemporary cultural studies, critical pedagogy, and activism. Books in the series will be of interest to interdisciplinary audiences in cultural studies, feminism, political theory, political economy, rhetoric and composition, postcolonial theory, transnational studies, literature, philosophy, sociology, Latino Studies, and many more.

Titles in Series:
Cultural Studies and the Corporate University, by Rachel Riedner and Kevin Mahoney
Democracies to Come: Rhetorical Action, Neoliberalism, and Communities of Resistance, by Rachel Riedner and Kevin Mahoney

Democracies to Come

Rhetorical Action, Neoliberalism, and Communities of Resistance

RACHEL RIEDNER AND KEVIN MAHONEY

Foreword by Susan Wells

LEXINGTON BOOKS

A division of
ROWMAN & LITTLEFIELD PUBLISHERS, INC.
Lanham • Boulder • New York • Toronto • Plymouth, UK

LEXINGTON BOOKS

A division of Rowman & Littlefield Publishers, Inc.
A wholly owned subsidiary of The Rowman & Littlefield Publishing Group, Inc.
4501 Forbes Boulevard, Suite 200
Lanham, MD 20706

Estover Road
Plymouth PL6 7PY
United Kingdom

British Library Cataloguing in Publication Information Available

Library of Congress Cataloging-in-Publication Data

Riedner, Rachel, 1966–
  Democracies to come : rhetorical action, neoliberalism, and communities of resistance /
Rachel Riedner and Kevin Mahoney.
      p. cm. — (Cultural studies/pedagogy/activism)
  Includes bibliographical references and index.
  ISBN-13: 978-0-7391-1104-8 (cloth : alk. paper)
  ISBN-10: 0-7391-1104-3 (cloth : alk. paper)
  1. Protest movements—Study and teaching. I. Mahoney, Kevin. II. Title.
  HN18.R429 2008
  322.4—dc22

                                                                              2008004135

Printed in the United States of America

⊖™ The paper used in this publication meets the minimum requirements of American
National Standard for Information Sciences—Permanence of Paper for Printed Library
Materials, ANSI/NISO Z39.48–1992.

To our families

Contents

Foreword
    Susan Wells, Temple University   ix

Preface   xiii

Acknowledgements   xvii

1   Introduction   1

2   Articulating Action in a Neoliberal World   17

3   Circulation of Affect in University Spaces   39

4   Circulation of Benevolence   51

5   Affective Intervention: Rhetorics of Despair and Hope   69

6   "The War for the Word Has Begun"   87

Bibliography   109

Index   117

About the Authors   121

Foreword

Kevin Mahoney and Rachel Riedner have written a book that urgently addresses our present moment, the moment of neoliberalism and the corporate university. I'd like to open a path into their book by invoking a quite different speech situation, the one faced by Augustine (yes, the saint) when, newly converted, he began preaching in fourth century North Africa. Trained in the elaborate rhetoric of figure and stasis developed by the migratory teachers of the Second Sophistic, still more than half in love with Cicero, Augustine faced a series of perplexing problems. Roman rhetoric, putatively developed to resolve the problems of a republic, never envisioned truly diverse audiences: the Roman orator spoke to the Senate, to the jury, and (rarely) to audiences of free Roman males. Augustine's new audience was male and female, free and slave, Roman and African and Greek and Berber, literate and illiterate. All of them needed to be addressed, instructed, moved, persuaded. In that bustling, prosperous world of late Roman North Africa, any sensible person would have imagined the Roman Empire going on indefinitely—after all, it had lasted hundreds of years, and survived any number of incursions. Any sensible person would have imagined the continuation of the empire's religious pluralism, with orthodox Christianity as the nominal imperial religion, but a continuing comfortable practice of indigenous North African religions, pagan cults, and all manner of irregular Christians—Manicheans, Donatists, Pelagians.

Augustine had other plans. He imagined a universal church, including virtually everyone, tolerating no other form of worship. Constructing such an institution would take hard rhetorical work: Augustine could not rely on imperial power to build the kind of consent that would make such a church into an effective institution. He would have to persuade. And so he turned to the tools at hand, the traditions of Greek and Roman rhetoric, for guidance. He freely discarded the elements of that tradition that did not suit his purpose: doctrinal instruction did not really require, or even much value, invention. Other elements of the rhetoric he had learned and taught seemed awkwardly frivolous—all those endless lists of tropes, for example. He used the tropes, deftly and to great effect, and dismissed the lists. Augustine did need to analyze different speech situations, to think about stylistic modulation, to consider the needs of various audiences: he found tools for this work in Cicero, argued for their use in Christian teaching, and offered successful models of rhetorically-informed teaching and preaching that influenced rhetorical practice for nearly a millennium. He sug-

ix

gested a way in which a public sphere, if a somewhat monologic public sphere, could be structured through religious discourse; for all his authoritarianism, Augustine was the first rhetorician to think seriously about how to win the assent of truly diverse audiences.

The rhetorical situation that Mahoney and Riedner face, that we face, is equally complex. We live in an imperial culture that claims democratic traditions; like Augustine's contemporaries, we may imagine ourselves in the last days of that empire, or be sure that it will last for centuries. The definitions of the public that Douglass, or Bryan, or even King took for granted won't work for us: besides face-to-face persuasion, our audiences connect through scores of new media; national publics have become mobile, and intersect with multinational organizations and forms of domination. Like Augustine, we survey this vexed scene, peer into the box of tools that various rhetorical traditions have constructed for us, and wonder what to leave behind, what to refunction, what to use. How can we construct a rhetoric for the discourses we encounter and for those we hope to produce? We are immersed in discourses that regulate markets on a global scale, that sponsor our participation in commodity systems, that contain and neutralize critical thought; we hope for discourses, both intimate and anonymous, wavering between scientific debate and political argument, never settling easily into received genres, that we work with our students to create.

In selecting from the rhetorical toolbox, Riedner and Mahoney have made wise choices. Without any cumbersome machinery of analysis, without any silly inventories of topics, they have chosen the most productive, the most efficacious, the most flexible, of the tools that rhetoric gives us. Let me list them:

- The notion of *kairos*, with all its marks of contingency, urgency, and immediacy. *Kairos*, for the Greeks, invoked the situation of the speaker as it pressed upon discourse: the famous statue of personified *kairos* by Lysippus showed an athlete pressing forward but poised. *Kairos* requires the rhetor to balance incongruous demands, to stay ahead of the batter (or runner), to reject solutions that worked once, but may not work again. The detailed and moving account in this book of the April 16, 2000 demonstrations against the International Monetary Fund in Washington, DC, is a wonderful analysis of a kairotic moment, its necessities, and its possibilities.
- Aristotle's available *means of persuasion*. A focus on the available means of persuasion grounds rhetorical intervention in our concrete discourse situation, and links our hope for rhetorical success to our ability to enter sympathetically the worlds of our audience. *Democracies to Come* takes seriously the location of rhetorical training in the university classroom: not all means of persuasion are available to us, as teachers, and those at hand are often compromised. Riedner and Mahoney also understand, however, the critical position of university

teachers as producers of a certain kind of labor power, and ask us to think through the possibilities of that location.

- The understanding of pedagogy as a culturally and politically consequential process, deeply implicated in social politics. Debates about pedagogy have haunted rhetorical instruction ever since Socrates hung around after Gorgias' speech to ask impolite questions. Sometimes, rhetorical training is rejected as debilitating—students who learn these fancy maneuvers won't be any good at the workaday writing and speaking they will need to do as adults. Or it can be seen as too habilitating—students who learn rhetorical tricks won't have any secure sense of what is really true or false. Both worries express a distrust of the tools of discourse, a recognition that the ability to see two sides of a case and to invent reasons is not a skill that can be contained once and for all. Since neoliberalism integrates rhetoric into its deepest productive struggles, a critical rhetorical education might prompt students to ask a very broad range of very impolite questions.

- The concept of a public (or counter-public) sphere, contested, flexible, and often quite degraded. Riedner and Mahoney's analysis of neoliberalism, of its construction of the market as the "arbiter of equality . . . the *definitive* democratic form of social organization" demonstrates how deeply compromised the public sphere that Habermas celebrated has become. Neoliberalism, which implies marginalization of those who do not fit the new world order, constructs very thin identities: it is possible to think of universities as sites where those identities can become thickened, mutually entangled, and engaged in rhetorical production outside the academy.

- An orientation to production, a refusal to see production as a minor matter of "application" or "technique." Taking up Susan Jarratt's critique of the analytic bias of cultural studies, Riedner and Mahoney advocate rhetorical instruction that helps students to counter the dominant discourse rather than simply opposing or negating it. They are willing to take up all the risks of this production; they share their experience bravely and frankly; they encourage courage and honesty in us, their readers.

- This commitment to production is evident throughout *Democracies to Come*, but especially in the discussion of rhetorical action: practices that create new literacies, new pedagogies, and new structures of feeling. The concept of rhetorical action helps us to move beyond pedagogies of propaganda and confrontation, and to consider what kinds of intervention will support the democratic forms we need now.

This book is not content, however, to refunction the venerable tools of rhetoric for the work of social resistance. In this volume, rhetorical concepts are brought together with the insights of new disciplines and ways of thinking. "Production" becomes a richer, less tractable concept when it includes reproduction, the social division of labor. The university is less idealized when understood as a specific late capitalist space, outsourcing its dining halls. Mahoney and Riedner demonstrate that this emerging field of study still provides a model for knowledge-making outside the structure of academic disciplines, still helps us identify areas of intervention and suggesting strategies for transformation. Augustine took a rhetorical theory adapted to trials and imperial courts and adapted it to the exigencies of preaching sermons, instructing converts, or disputing on matters of doctrine—not an easy task. This book adapts a rhetoric oriented to the production of academic papers, technical reports, and the odd op-ed piece to the exigencies of quite different genres: talk shows, websites, official documents, ephemeral texts.

It is speculative in the best sense—it offers a sense that our common, daily practice of teaching writing could become quite different. The classroom possibilities that Kevin and Rachel explore are exciting, risky, and entirely possible. They are honest in acknowledging the limits and difficulties of their pedagogies, and they insist on the contingency of the spaces they have created, the fragility of the alliances they have forged. Augustine proposed a rhetoric for "a strong people," hoping, of course, to unite his auditors, confirm their belief, and make them strong. Mahoney and Riedner are writing a rhetoric for curious people, "epistemologically curious" people. They hope to provoke their readers, incite readers in their own investigations, support them in their own interventions. All of us have reason to share these hopes, and to be grateful to these writers for their work.

Susan Wells
Professor of English
Temple University

Preface

Democracies to Come: Rhetorical Action, Neoliberalism, and Communities of Resistance draws upon a variety of contemporary sites and moments (e.g. IMF/World Bank protests, writing emerging from social movements in struggle against neoliberalism, classroom praxis, postcolonial literature, student activism) to explore new relationships—pedagogical, emotional, affective, and social—that can be the basis of new political and social organizing. *Democracies to Come*, and the Lexington Press series Cultural Studies/Pedagogy/Activism it inaugurates, seeks to pose and imagine exigencies within the current neoliberal hegemony. While this is not a book that is "about" neoliberalism in the sense that we map its rhetorical, cultural, and political formations, this work is bound up in the particular conjuncture of neoliberalism. Our purpose is to create pedagogical responses that articulate the contingencies and affinities of the particular moment. In that respect, our motives are rhetorical in the strong sense of the word. That is, we write to intervene in the present, knowing that our intervention will necessarily be incomplete, partial. Our intervention calls for responses and is, itself, contingent.

In each chapter of the book we ask: How can pedagogy be conceptualized as a site in which to intervene in culture and to act politically? How can pedagogy help cultivate the *kairotic* act of opening spaces for inquiring into the social relations that education helps shape? How can we re-imagine practices capable of contextualizing education within larger educational and market forces? How do we develop the desire and habit to recognize moments when we move beyond norms and develop new ways of seeing, acting, and relating? How do we see pedagogical activism not as an end in itself but as an integral process of revitalizing democracy? How to create moments to process new arguments, respond to particular conjunctures, and create new languages that articulate the contingencies and affinities of the particular moment?

Initially drawing upon our involvement with and observations of IMF/World Bank protests in Washington, DC, the introductory chapter investigates pedagogy as a cultural literacy which intervenes in a multiplicity of systems, institutions, formations, and constituencies to create meaning. This chapter

begins a discussion of emergent feelings and emotions that put us in communication and solidarity with others. Our discussion of emotion and feeling is extended in subsequent chapters and leads to a discussion of affect in the final
chapter.

Our introduction also begins a discussion of democracy and democratic
practice linked to pedagogy. We approach pedagogy as a space of learning—not
simply "teaching"—whose purpose is to develop an understanding of social
structures and networks and in so doing develop critical literacies for democracies to come. Approached in this way, pedagogy becomes a cultural force for
democracy in its own right; a cultural literacy, which intervenes in a multiplicity
of systems, institutions, formations, and constituencies to create meaning. As a
practice of meaning-making, pedagogy becomes rhetorical action: a political
practice of making, reproducing, and remaking of social relations, identities, and
intervening in relations of dominance and exploitation. The protests against the
IMF/World Bank, like many of the recent global justice protests, offered a vision of innovation, celebration, and difference in their conceptions of political
participation and in their rhetoric. Through our discussion of the protests we ask:
How do we actively understand and feel democracy not as established in advance but, as Judith Butler suggests, as something to be undergone, like a passion must be undergone, a process of becoming, not something achieved in the
past and therefore finished/done? How can we nurture the languages and practices evident in those protests—protests in which affective experiences and practices became moments of new possibility, of lived solidarity?

The second chapter looks at universities in the current moment, investigating the material and discursive contexts for pedagogy. Our work in this chapter goes beyond characterizing the current conjunctural moment—what we'll
call neoliberalism—to the potentials for rhetorical action that this moment offers.
In this chapter, we're interested in the ways in which neoliberal rhetorics are
persuasive inasmuch as they craft and direct our modes of life, languages
through which we make ourselves and our world, and, in the context of neoliberalism, languages that can be mobilized for new understandings and new modes
of life. We examine pedagogical sites, relationships, and possibilities that are in
excess of the institution of the university or sites within the university that are in
excess of its operations within neoliberalism. Chapter 2 continues to develop the
key term of this book, rhetorical action, here an intervention into literate spaces
in order to work toward more effective modes of interventions—interventions
that seek out cracks, openings, and gaps in neoliberal hegemony.

The third chapter explains our focus on conjunctural moments, crisis of
hegemony or crisis in the coordination and maintenance of voluntary social alliances that ensure antagonistic classes internalize a set of perceived common
sense interests and emotions. As Stuart Hall says, we investigate the "particular
configuration of a conjuncture," in order to create literate possibilities. In this
case, our example comes from an event where student protestors were arrested
in the student center where one of us teaches. In the context of these arrests, we
ask with Hall "what does this have to do with everything else" in the interest of

creating articulations that can become the openings for rhetorical possibilities ("Plenary Address"). From this standpoint, the crisis of hegemony is not something one has to wait for to emerge. The exigence is not just something that we respond to. Rather, it's already there: the work of connecting, these linkages allow us to see where the crisis in hegemony is in any particular moment.

In the fourth and fifth chapters, we explore emotions as, on the one hand, obstacles to pedagogical inquiry and, on the other, as the site of rhetorical action. Both these chapters open up rhetoric into an analysis of the "strong" emotions that characterize neoliberalism and that make collective action and experience possible. The fourth chapter investigates benevolence as part of the material framework of colonialism. Locating benevolence in several cultural locations, tracking the rhetoric of benevolence allows us to locate global in the local and personal. The fifth chapter addresses dominant argumentative structures that cultivate affects of despair and hopelessness, reproducing neoliberal power relations. Not only are neoliberal power relations reproduced, they become internalized, displacing public democratic deliberation with private moral negotiation. The movement of these two chapters is to identify relationships and common experiences that are in excess of familiar emotions that can function as a form of social power even while not being recognized as such. These nascent emotional connections are, as our introductory narrative on the IMF/World Bank protests suggests, potential sites of political, cultural, and activist work.

In both the fourth and fifth chapters, there is a movement from the emergent, that which is oppositional to the dominant hegemony, to the pre-emergent, that which is not yet given a language, narrative, or incorporated into the dominant. Working with Zapatista writing and writing by cultural studies scholars, the sixth chapter moves from an analysis of identifiable narratives to a discussion of the possibilities for affective openings. This chapter argues for a political linkage between two rhetorical traditions, a cultural studies' tradition situated primarily within universities, and a practice of political communities in activist struggle. These traditions emerge from different locations, but they both situate rhetoric as action, that is, a pedagogical effort that is a means to create and remake democracy. This work, as we argue, requires a re-articulation of the whole complex of social relations—productive and reproductive labor, structures of feeling, identities, agency, voice, and democratic participation. This complete re-articulation sets the stage for intervention in rhetorical spaces that are fundamental for a democracy to come.

As a closing note, we want to draw attention to the genre from which this book draws its critical direction. While *Democracies to Come* is a book, its energy is that of the essay. In his article "The Essay as Form," Theodore Adorno showed his impatience with the German "customary national prejudice" of denigrating the essay (151). He suggests that the academic guild privileges "the universal, the everlasting," and resists the essay "because it is reminiscent of the academic freedom that, from the time of an unsuccessful and lukewarm Enlightenment, since Leibniz's day, all the way to the present has never really emerged" (152). The essay, argues Adorno,

> does not permit its domain to be prescribed. Instead of achieving something scientifically, or creating something artistically, the effort of the essay reflects a childlike freedom that catches fire, without scruple, on what others have already done. The essay mirrors what is loved and hated instead of presenting the intellect, on the model of a boundless work ethic, as *creatio ex nihilo*. It does not begin with Adam and Eve but with what it wants to discuss; it says what is at issue and stops where it feels itself complete—not where nothing is left to say (152).

The essay, from our perspective, privileges the conjunctural and the contingent. Its aim is to engage, to provoke, to encourage further conversation. It is marked historically by a sense of urgency to say something, to have a say, to respond, to provoke, to claim, and to disrupt.

It seems that the essay—or the energy of the essay at least—appeals more and more to those who are taking on neoliberalism and seeking to reach across borders to build an alternative to neoliberal globalization. Pierre Bourdieu, for example, has produced two short books, *Acts of Resistance: Against the Tyranny of the Market* and *Firing Back: Against the Tyranny of the Market*, that abandon the deep theoretical language of *Distinction* or *An Outline of a Theory of Practice*. Novelist and global justice activist Arundhati Roy's short books (e.g. *War Talk, An Ordinary Person's Guide to Empire*, and *Power Politics*) continue to be staples for global justice activists. Judith Butler and Gayatri Chakravorty Spivak's recently published conversation, *Who Sings the Nation-State?*, also seeks a form that crosses formal boundaries, without scruple, refusing their domain to be prescribed. Perhaps the essay, or better "the essay," speaks more to Judith Butler's spirit of a democracy to come: "Democracy does not speak in unison; its tunes are dissonant, and necessarily so. It is not a predictable process; it must be undergone, like a passion must be undergone" (39).

It is with such passion that we offer this book.

Acknowledgements

The idea of this book began in the former Writing Program at The George Washington University. Directed by Dan Moshenberg, this Writing Program created solidarity around activism that continue to resonate with us as we have moved on to different institutions and positions. In reading groups, union organizing, hall conversations, discussions after work over beer, and barbecues, emerged a community of friends centered around collaboration and activism that continues to sustain our thinking, teaching, and activism. From that rich and vibrant period there are many people who deeply influenced this book that we need to thank: in addition to Dan Moshenberg, we thank Angela Hewett, Robert Mcruer, Phyllis Ryder, Randi Kristensen, Samantha Murphy, Justin Roby, Zak Wolfe, Abby Wilkerson, Mark Mullen, Carol Hayes, Andrea Levine, Noreen O'Conner, Rich Hancuff, Pam Presser, and, for all his support and encouragement, Steve Velasquez. Rachel also thanks the faculty and students from the Program in the Human Sciences, most significantly Gail Weiss and Alf Hiltebeitel, and faculty and students in the Women's Studies Program at GW. She also thanks Laurie Geller, Jeff Becan, and Cedric Yeh for their friendship.

After Kevin left GW for Kutztown, the Writing Program was removed from the English Department. That difficult transition brought Rachel new colleagues, including Gustavo Guerra, Eric Drown, Phillip Troutman, Sandie Friedman, Cayo Gamber, Ariane Chernock, Heather Schell, and Christy Zink. Rachel particularly thanks her office mate, Gustavo, for putting up with a cluttered office while this book was being written and his commitment to academic freedom. I thank Phyllis Ryder, for her leadership and vision in the new writing program, Robert Mcruer for his commitment to writing beyond institutional boundaries, and Cathy Eisenhower, for her friendship, wackiness, and collegiality. Finally, I thank the members of the Cultural Studies in a Time of Danger Reading group, Jason Hipp, Aliya Weiss, Ned Mitchell, and Robert Mcruer.

Kevin's move to Kutztown brought the promise of being part of a unionized faculty in the midst of adjusting to a neoliberal academic environment, an English department facing many retirements and curricular change, and a new city, Allentown, in which to build new alliances. At Kutztown, I wish to think Janice Chernekoff for her tremendous mentorship and sense of patience, fairness, and long-term thinking; Linda Cullum, the "third musketeer" in our Composition group; Judy Kennedy, for being willing to move through arguments to become a key supporter; Walt Nott (who became a member of the English Department) and Carl Brunner from the Dean's Office who helped steer me away from potential landmines during activist and union campaigns. Walt Nott, my dear friend, comrade, and "family," I will miss you daily. In addition, I would like to thank Aaron Barlow, Jennifer Forsyth, and Amy Lynch-Biniek for being a joy to work with collaboratively; and, importantly, Jennifer Bottinelli, who has not only been a good colleague, but who also introduced me to my wife, Chris Kilczewski. Most importantly, I want to thank my wife Chris "mucho" for her support, love, and patience.

At Kutztown, I have also been privileged to work with an amazing group of colleagues who have dedicated their time, voices, and energies to revitalize our local chapter of the Association of Pennsylvania College and University Faculty (APSCUF): Kristin Bremer, Jim Delle, Ken Ehrensal, Mike Gambone, Ted Hickman, Will Jefferson, Paul Quinn, John Riley, and Anke Walz. Many of these people committed themselves to building a new, active union despite their status of junior and/or temporary faculty.

I am eternally grateful for the amazing group of graduate students and faculty at Miami University who gave me a concrete experience of what a rigorous, committed, and political academic community was like. Thanks especially to Rich Zumkhawala-Cook, Scott Lyons, and Pegeen and Doug Reichert Powell. Special thanks to Pegeen and Doug for being a model for a loving, committed, political relationship. Thanks to Kate Ronald, Susan Jarratt, Mary Jean Corbett, and Mary Cayton for their invaluable contributions and responses to my dissertation and academic work. Their words of advice and encouragement continue to stay with me today.

We are especially grateful to Rob Carley from Lexington Press who noticed this project when it was a two sentence description of a conference paper at the Cultural Studies Association annual conference. His encouragement and support has made this book and the series it initiates possible. When Rob left Lexington for Texas, we were serendipitously assigned Joseph Parry as our editor and contact at Lexington. We also thank him for his support. John Trimbur provided a sharp and generous review of this book which enabled us to see more clearly its contributions to rhetoric and writing studies. We thank him for making himself available to us during the revision process.

Rachel thanks Kevin for his generosity, patience, and commitment to activism. It has been an absolute pleasure to co-write this book. Kevin thanks Rachel for her energy, kindness, joy, tremendous patience, and her willingness to stick with this project at times when the demands of teaching a 4-4 load, union organizing, and committee work left me wanting for time to write consistently. The experience of writing this book with her has been, indeed, a pleasure.

Rachel thanks the wonderful childcare providers who take care of Gabriella and Sam while she works and writes. She particularly thanks Lena Sawah,

Denise Culkin, and all the fabulous teachers at the Smithsonian Early Enrichment Center:

While this book was under construction, our families grew. Kevin married Chris in Allentown. Young Sam was born in Washington, DC, and Rachel, Steve, and big sister Gabriella celebrated his birth. While this book was being written, Rachel and Steve's family lost our beautiful, strong minded niece, Cristina Fury, whom we remember everyday.

We dedicate this book to our families. In Silver Spring, Maryland, Steve, Gabriella, and Sam; and grandparents, aunts, uncles, and cousins in Boston and Wooster, Ohio. Special thanks to all the writers in Rachel's family who have encouraged this project. In Allentown, Pennsylvania, to Chris and Finnegan and to parents, sisters, brothers, in-laws, and nieces and nephews in Utica and New Hartford, New York, and Warminster, Chalfont, and Perkasie, Pennsylvania.

Portions of chapter 3 first appeared in the *minnesota review*, reprinted here with permission. Sections of chapters 4 and 6 appear in Rachel's article, "Affective Encounters," in the *Journal of Advanced Composition*, reprinted here with permission.

Cover image design credit (top): Max Fox

Cover photo credit (bottom): Steve Velasquez

Chapter 1
Introduction

For creativity and social self-creation are both known and unknown events and it is still from grasping the known that the unknown—the next step, the next work, is conceived. (Williams, *Marxism and Literature*, 212)

What I'm telling you happened fifteen years ago. Thirty years ago, a few people scratched history, and knowing this, they began calling to many others so that, by dint of scribbling, scratching, and scrawling, they would end up rending the veil of history, so that the light would finally be seen. That, and nothing else, is the struggle we are making. And so if you ask us what we want, we will unashamedly answer: "To open a crack in history." (Marcos, *Our Word Is Our Weapon*, 216)

It may be that what is right and what is good consist in staying open to the tensions that beset the most fundamental categories we require, in knowing unknowingness at the core of what we know, and what we need, and in recognizing the sign of life in what we undergo without certainty about what will come. (Judith Butler, *Undoing Gender*, 39)

Introduction

During the weekend of April 16, 2000 (hereafter referred to as A-16), tens of thousands of international protesters gathered in Washington, DC to disrupt the annual meeting of the International Monetary Fund (IMF). Approximately thirty-five thousand protestors arrived in the DC streets where The George Washington University is located, the institution where at the time we were both

1

teaching in the writing program. The protestors included a diverse and intersecting range of groups from all over the world: labor unions, feminists, anti-
capitalist groups, queer activists, supporters of environmental issues, supporters
of indigenous peoples, students, mothers of the "disappeared" in South America,
anarchists, black bloc members, and many others (Ryder).

The weekend was marked by both carnevalesque joy and violent
clashes with the police. Protestors danced and marched through the streets with
large puppets and banners, sometimes clashing with police, sometimes attacked
by police. There were protestors carrying a huge papier-mâché sea turtle; a web
of string was used to symbolically barricade an intersection that led to the World
Bank; black bloc members carried signs with quotations by Emma Goldman,
and radical cheer leaders sang and performed protest chants. There were also
moments of violence. On Sunday afternoon at the corner of 21st and G streets a
large group of protestors was locked down in the center of the intersection surrounded by groups of supporters. A police bus drove in; District police officers
emptied out of it and attacked the protestors with batons. None of the protestors,
as we observed it, did anything to provoke this attack. The crowd surrounding
the protestors shouted "peace, peace," and converged upon the intersection. The
police then withdrew back to their bus and left. As the police departed, protestors and onlookers spontaneously danced in the intersection.

There was a moment in the midst of this confrontation that seemed to
pass in slow motion. The police and National Guard converged on the group of
protestors blocking the intersection and three armored vehicles made their way
to the front of the barricades. Warnings to disperse by the police echoed off the
corporate, government, and university buildings as inaudible white noise from
battery enhanced blow-horns. Black clad riot police surrounded the protestors,
taking up lines behind cattle barricades, each fully clad in body armor, armed
with batons, clear plastic shields, and gas masks. On a cue heard or seen only by
the riot police, they all donned and secured gas masks over their noses and
mouths. Several National Guard soldiers emerged atop the armored vehicles,
loaded their tear-gas launchers and rubber bullet guns and aimed squarely into
the heart of the crowd. Police on the lines, sweat dripping down the parts of their
faces not covered by the gas masks, were a multicultural mix of State power—a
statement of the contradictions of capital and the limited choices for advancement for this urban, non-white majority of the nation's capital. Drums from
within the ranks of the protestors grew louder. Several protestors motioned for
the crowd to sit down…to raise two fingers high above their heads as signs of
peace. All motion seemed to stop, locked in this tense standoff. You could see a
mix of fear and resolve, tears and love, on the faces of the growing number of
people sitting down in the intersection in the shadow of the glistening façade of
the World Bank's international headquarters.

Peace-signing hands met the gaze of tear-gas and rubber-bullet guns,
the crowd anticipating what seemed like an inevitable order to fire from some
observation post on one of the roofs or balconies of the surrounding buildings.
But the order never came. When that first soldier atop one of the armored vehi-

cles lowered his gun and lifted his mask, you could feel in the crowd a tangible, visceral sense that they, we, had won this particular battle against neoliberalism. On this day, at this location, no more tear gas would be fired. The armored vehicles withdrew. The faces of the riot police surrounding the protesters began to emerge from their gas masks. And the drums and chants grew into a celebration. Tension and fear gave way to joy. At a debriefing in the following days, a GW student talked about his years of cynicism, that nothing could be done in the face of the global march of capital. But that feeling changed for him during the standoff. That moment on the corner of 21st and G Streets, he said, was the first time that he *felt* part of something in his life.

This convergence of celebration, violence, innovation, complex and intersecting identities, and a heterogeneity of ideas, people, and perspectives took place in and around the neighborhood and campus where both of us lived and taught. Because of the influx of masses of protestors who vowed to disrupt the World Bank and IMF meetings, the university canceled classes, and that weekend a great many students and faculty, warned by the university and the media of street violence, stayed away from campus. This moment that took place in our local public space, our campus and our homes, was at the same time an event that was part of the momentum of the anti-globalization movement that appeared on the North American scene most visible at the protest in Seattle against the WTO in late November 1999. Because the protest took place in our local public space, it provided us a specific opportunity, an exigence, to think through the protests as a pedagogical moment, a moment for thinking through the intimate connections between activist organization and emergent practices of democracy.

As this opening narrative suggests, in *Democracies to Come*, we explore the nexus of practices for learning, sites of intervention, and political possibilities that enable us to recast, to reimagine, our relationships to power, political organization, and the meaning of pedagogy at this historical conjuncture. Pedagogy, as we understand it, is a practice of learning that creates ways of knowing that suggest political possibilities. Pedagogy is a praxis of learning strategies for intervening, reassembling, and inventing sustainable relationships of solidarity, networks of affinity, that hold out the possibility of countering neoliberal hegemony. And pedagogy is always inscribed in a particular context, a particular conjunctural moment.

Democracies to Come draws upon a variety of cultural spaces, including activist movements, classroom practice, and cultural locations where normative social formations are challenged. We are interested in mapping emergent political formations that create pedagogical meaning; that is, political formations that offer us languages of knowing, understanding, and learning. A-16, and other examples that we explore throughout the book, blur traditional boundaries between spaces of activism, pedagogy, theory, culture, and rhetoric. For us, action and engagement are spaces of learning, spaces of learning are spaces of action and engagement, and ways of knowing are languages of political action.

Our purpose is to extend discussions of critical pedagogy into broader contexts of democratic struggle, extending well beyond and across the classroom walls of academe. The following questions suggest a nexus between pedagogy and democracy: How does action become a moment of and for pedagogy, that is, how does educational praxis respond to a particular cultural moment? If we are committed to deepening and expanding vocabularies for new, critical perspectives and for expanding democratic participation, what pedagogical strategies can help us understand the moment of globalization that we're in? How do we reframe our existing conceptual frameworks, walk different rhetorical pathways, and in so doing create a "new place" in the "non-place" of Empire?

Genesis of the Project: Many Words Walk in the World

The events of A-16 created a moment—an experience that for us was actively lived and felt—that brought together the political and the pedagogical, rhetorical, and theoretical. For each of us, the events of A-16 began long conversations, reading, talking, and thinking about pedagogy as a public, democratic practice that exceeds the bounds of the classroom and the university space and establishes affective relations that sustain and create new networks of affinity that are the life-blood of social movements.

What was going on in the streets of DC on A-16 was a mass and collective pedagogical moment as much as it was an explicit act of resistance to neoliberal capital. We were witnessing the birth of movement whose goal was nothing short of the creation of new political formations, pedagogical relationships that opened new political possibilities for counter-hegemonic organization. For us, A-16 was an emergent moment that "open[ed] a crack in history" (Marcos 216). A-16 posed questions about alternative and oppositional political practices as well as significant questions about the conjuncture between pedagogical practices and these emergent political movements. We asked ourselves: What's the connection between what we do in the classroom and this emergent political formation? How do we, joining the work in which these social movements were already doing, begin rethinking pedagogy and political action as simultaneously global, personal, and local?

A-16 was also an occasion to think about the role of the university in a globalizing world. In academic spaces—which, as Chandra Mohanty points out, are "contradictory place[s] where knowledges are colonized but also contested"—what is a praxis of critique and intervention? (*Feminism Without Borders*, 170). Universities are often sites in which the economic and political interests of a dominant class are consolidated through pedagogical practices that shape identities, behaviors, and feelings. But, as we will argue, in the second chapter, universities are also spaces that often exceed their role in securing the hegemonic order.

We also began to think through the practice and meaning of democracy in a neoliberal world. While the protestors offered a vision of innovation, celebration, and difference in their conceptions of political participation and in their rhetoric, for many students, faculty, and others it is difficult to see the critical possibilities that the protests provide because of the belief that democracy has already been assured by other means. As Angela Hewett argues, where our public discourses continue to reinforce the notion that we already live in a free and fair society, and that the government, police, and institutions of civil society protect these freedoms, the dialogue and innovation that the protests offer are not recognized as democratic. In this discursive and ideological context, it is difficult to see the protests as anything else but "disruptive, illegal, a violation of democratic principles" (Hewett).

We saw the protests as an opportunity to move students from what Paolo Freire calls "ingenuous curiosity" to "epistemological curiosity." In *Pedagogy of Freedom*, Freire argues that:

> human curiosity, as a phenomenon present to all vital experience, is in a permanent process of social and historical construction and reconstruction. It's precisely because ingenuous curiosity does not automatically become critical that one of the essential tasks of progressive educational praxis is the promotion of a curiosity that is critical, bold, and adventurous. (*Pedagogy of Freedom*, 38)

The events of A-16 were an occasion to engage the nexus of power/authority, citizenship/democracy, violence/celebration, critical curiosity/hope all brought to the surface by an incomplete yet advancing process of neoliberal globalization. These conjunctions resonate for us, suggesting that our understanding of pedagogy, of academic work, and political praxis needs to be rearticulated in the context of these new social movements.

The idea that we already live in a free and fair society and the difficulty of recognizing as democratic anything but the official state operations is echoed in the discourse of the media. Mainstream media characterized the A-16 protestors as outside of these democratic institutions, repeating the dominant discourse and upholding the authority of the state. What these characterizations *failed* to capture gave the official media accounts a feeling of one too many sequels. We're not only arguing that the media simply got it wrong (yes, they did); we're arguing that because of the discursive and political frameworks through which they read the protests, they couldn't but get it wrong. As Judith Butler says about democracy, "It may also be that life itself becomes foreclosed when the right way is decided in advance, we impose what is right for everyone without finding a way to enter into community, and discover there the 'right' in the midst of cultural translation" (39). The protests were, after all, in English so problems of translation of so many U.S. newspapers were not a linguistic barrier. But there was a discursive barrier.

The mainstream media put the protests into the wrong frame, the wrong structure of knowing, a re-run of past protests, so that the feelings provoked by the protests were completely missed, not possible within the representative framework of their discourse. As our colleague Phyllis Ryder notes:

> Much can be made of the way the media characterized the event . . . some editorials decried the protestors as throwbacks from the sixties who sought to march simply for the sake of marching, or as "young, alienated, anarchist youth." Some newspapers, comparing the events to Seattle, disparaged the activists and called the protests a "failure" because they did not shut down the meeting. Others noted that the activists had disrupted the meetings but scolded them for not producing a coherent message for public consumption . . . Other arguments suggest that despite these results, the protest was not a success because its goal was too loosely stated. (21)

The misrepresentation and misunderstanding of these strategies of intervention in mainstream media notwithstanding, in our teaching and our writing, A-16 encouraged us to explore "a curiosity that is critical, bold and adventurous" (Freire, *Pedagogy of Freedom*, 38). This curiosity began with interest in critical literacy of the moment. A-16 compelled us to search for languages which could articulate ideas of protest, democracy, identity, and violence that we saw, experienced, and felt throughout the weekend.

In the long term, the protests continue to resonate for us as we think through the opportunities that they offer. How can epistemological curiosity be sustained? How do we actively understand and feel democracy not as established in advance but as what Judith Butler refers to as something to be undergone, like a passion must be undergone, a process of becoming, not something achieved in the past and therefore finished/done? How can we sustain the language and practice that the protests offered where affective experiences become the basis of lived solidarities?

What's the Word?:
Finding a Political Vocabulary Within and Against Empire

These questions are particularly pressing in the context of an absence of vocabulary adequate to the task of representing and embodying the slippage between the carnevalesque and violence, the heterogeneity of identities of "democracy to come," and the nexus of feeling, thought and experience. In their work *Empire*, Michael Hardt and Antonio Negri advocate for new vocabularies and practices to respond to the new world order. Hardt and Negri argue that the new social and political space of Empire is marked by an absence of vocabulary that is adequate to the task of mapping and articulating the increasingly complex and diverse nature of the phenomenon that we call globalization. This absence is a central concern in *Empire* because networks of relations of global capital have out-paced our language for grasping the resultant dynamics and because the latest stage of capital effectively incorporates hybridity, flexibility, and difference.

Hardt and Negri suggest that the political task of giving "name to what is already going on" is not just a task of political theory. They argue that the task of acquiring a theoretical vocabulary to grasp the current moment is a pedagogical task. Learning about local/global (and we'll complicate the notion of the local in the second chapter) efforts, they argue, gives us a critical ability to develop new political strategies: "simply by considering a proposal one gains a new, critical perspective on the existing structures, something like a cognitive map of the global system. Each proposal, in this sense, is a pedagogical tool. Every person who thinks, 'That's a good idea, why can't we do that?' *learns* an important lesson" (306, our italics).

In the current moment, in the moment of Empire, in the moment of neoliberalism, pedagogy becomes a space of learning whose purpose is to develop an understanding of new structures and in so doing develop literacies for new, critical perspectives for democracies to come. If we think about pedagogy in this way, it becomes a cultural force for democracy in its own right; a cultural literacy, which intervenes in a multiplicity of systems, institutions, formations, and constituencies to create meaning. As a practice of meaning-making, pedagogy becomes *rhetorical action*: a political practice of making, reproducing, and remaking of social relations, identities, and intervening in relations of dominance and exploitation. In this context, as Diana George argues in "A Matter of Life and Death: Public Debate in the Culture of Consent," the study of how to best intervene in literate spaces is fundamental to democratic participation—even more so in times of crisis. As George suggests, our current context is not a time to be disabled by a failure of vocabulary; rather, "it's a great time to be a rhetorician." That is, rhetorical practice is well-suited to opening spaces and nurturing possibilities for new discursive formations.

Hardt and Negri's idea of learning can be expanded into our discussion of pedagogy. But how does a person shift from her or his current mode of thinking to Hardt and Negri's notion of learning? That is, what are the conditions that lead someone to say: "That's a good idea, why can't we do that?" Openness to learning—what Gayatri Spivak calls "learning to learn from below"—is not decided in advance; it is a framework, a feeling, a relationship that must be created rather than assumed (Angus). We can think about learning, as the cynical student from GW recognized, as an emotional process. As Sara Ahmed suggests in *The Cultural Politics of Emotion*, emotions persuade people at the local level, and, therefore, can be the site of political work. Ahmed's work on emotion enables us to ask: How can emotions become the site of collective politics? Can we see emotions as pedagogical, that is, offering us languages of knowing, understanding and learning? How can we understand emotion as the site of literacy?

Our identities and literacies are formed (and this is an ongoing process) through complex cultural, educational systems that include media, social practices, domestic situations and "State" apparatuses. We extend the term learning from Hardt and Negri into emotion as a way of knowing, experiencing. A-16 is a moment of intersubjective learning that is *felt* as the GW student explained. This feeling puts us in communication and solidarity with others, directly connecting us to others in ways that are not strictly about others. It is not about saying we know others or can translate these feelings directly. It is a collective experience of lived pedagogy where knowledge, experience, theory, and practice are relational. In all chapters of this book, therefore, we consider emotion as part of the whole process of learning (to rephrase Raymond Williams).

Emotions, therefore, are sites of political work. We can study and create critical rhetoric that pays attention, as Susan Jarratt suggests, to who is feeling, who feels on behalf of whom, who is listening (or not listening) to these feelings and how these feelings are listened to ("Beside Ourselves," 57). We can study how feelings are seen as personal and unpack their relationship to larger social contexts, hierarchies, emergent forms, and dominant characteristics, the work of theory. We can trace the internal logic of feelings, analyze their structure, and track their relationship to "formal or systemic beliefs" and intuitions. In so doing, we can develop a rhetoric that articulates emotion as thought and articulates emotion as common. Emotions are an opening into the social and material world: they are therefore the sites of political and cultural work and the possible site of the formation of class, the work of activism.

Situated Cultural Rhetorics: The Next Step

In *Democracies to Come*, and the series that it inaugurates, the lived and felt understandings of the new world order become the basis for our discussion of rhetorical action. But, before we discuss this new world order, some words about "disciplinary" location. *Democracies to Come* may not be immediately recognizable as either a cultural studies text or a rhetoric and composition text because it doesn't directly address contemporary debates and developments of specific concern to the fields as defined in scholarly publications and conversations.[1] However, if this book helps revitalize cultural studies traditions, it does so by revisiting the ideas upon which all current scholarly work in the field is based: everyday practices of social change within local and situated conjunctures. If it helps revitalize rhetoric and composition, it does so by revisiting pedagogy, strategies of learning that emerge from contingent moments and situated rhetorical exigencies.

Our text emerges from intersections among cultural rhetorics, new work on globalization and "Empire," and public pedagogies and rhetorics. We seek to broaden conceptions of pedagogy from an institutionalized system of instruction to broader, dynamic sites at the intersections between theory and practice. We hope to expand concepts of pedagogy for the purpose of expanding democratic and liberatory spaces of freedom. Not a pedagogy of credentialing or submission but, as Paulo Freire argues, a pedagogy of freedom.

To explain this in a different way, our text does not directly engage traditions of cultural studies that might be expected from a book called "rethinking cultural studies," we're not rethinking or critiquing the Frankfurt School or the Birmingham School although this work and these traditions underlie our point of departure: everyday practices, emotions, affects, and contemporary conditions of capital. An analogy for how we think about this text's relationship to cultural studies might look to Gramsci's *Prison Notebooks*' relationship to marxist theory.: Gramsci assumes historical materialism and specific marxist revolutionary struggles as he attempts to work through new forms of state and civil society that are emerging in the pre–World War II era. That is, he does not write about or explain historical materialism. Rather he "writes out of" historical materialism and revolutionary struggles. Historical materialism and revolutionary struggle are contexts for his scholarship.

In the same way, our understanding of pedagogy assumes, "writes out of," Paulo Freire's pedagogy for liberation. Freire argues for pedagogy as the expansion and extension of human agency to all peoples. Such a position necessitates a close consideration of the intersections among literacy, power, capital, and, we'll add, emotion. So, for us, cultural studies and its traditions, its expansion into areas like emotion, is the context through which we embark upon a discussion of rhetorical action as pedagogy in the second chapter.

Our discussion of pedagogy also calls upon Derrida's discussions of democracy, particularly the ways we are thinking about rhetorical action in the final chapter. Following, Derrida's argument, we're thinking of democracy not in the narrow context of its current nation-state structure of representational or participatory democracy. In Derrida's later work, particularly *Rogues, Negotiations*, and *Politics of Friendship*, democracy is not a system, a government, or an ideal. Nor is it temporal, something we're working towards in the current structure. It is closely related to Derrida's notion of *différance*, the impossibility of closing off or deferring meaning in language, the possibility of differentiation or, even opposition (38). As Derrida argues, following Benjamin, "there is not yet any democracy worthy of this name. Democracy *remains* to come: to engender or to regenerate . . . it will always remain to come, it will never be present in the present, it will never present itself, will never come, will remain always to come, like the impossible itself" (82 and 73).

As our invocation of scholars such as Freire, Gramsci, and Derrida suggests, *Democracies to Come* emerges from a disciplinary conversation between the fields of cultural studies and rhetoric and composition. As we've brought together the terms pedagogy, rhetorical action, rhetoric, theory, and democracy, part of our purpose is to create lines of affinity between these two fields. Rhetoric—with its charge to articulate languages of and for the moment—has much in common with cultural studies, with its emphasis on the conditions of discursive production. Rhetoric offers cultural studies a particular focus on timely action. Composition, the other half of the disciplinary dyad, has a long interest in pedagogy. The Freirian tradition talks about learning as a practice of and for freedom. Cultural studies shares these interests in articulation, in its emphasis on hegemony and power, in finding theoretical languages to uncovers modes of domination, and its interest in examining formations of the current conjuncture. At the nexus of these fields, we find desire to create practices for learning, emergent and pre-emergent languages of disruption (theoretical or otherwise) that create exigencies—critical possibilities—for the current moment, neoliberalism. In chapters throughout the book, we call this concept rhetorical action.

Current Context

This new world order, as we will discuss in the following chapter, we are calling neoliberalism: an economic policy of upward redistribution in which public services are privatized, markets are opened up, and weakened government regulations are allowing corporations the "freedom" to pursue capital by extending market relations ever deeper into our social relations.[2] Neoliberalism is also a rhetoric, what Pierre Bourdieu calls a "strong" rhetoric, a discourse of public persuasion that is embedded in the particular relations between State and capitalist power (what Hardt and Negri call Empire).[3] This is not persuasion in the classical sense of rhetoric, but persuasion as a mode of authoritative discourse, particularly the authoritative discourse of Empire, that is enacted materially, on bodies, practices, subjectivities, cultures, and communities. Neoliberalism is the pedagogy of Empire.

In this sense, neoliberalism is the means through which consent is achieved in this new world order. Consent, according to Antonio Gramsci, is possible only given the threat of State violence: Gramsci understands consent as "'historically' caused by the prestige (and consequent confidence) which the dominant group enjoys because of its position and function in the world of production," where the "apparatus of state coercive power" is held in reserve to enforce "discipline on those groups who do not 'consent' either actively or passively" (*Prison Notebooks*, 12). As the pedagogy of Empire, neoliberalism is effective *as a pedagogy* insofar as it remains "hidden" *as a pedagogy*, as a historically specific rhetoric charged with "teaching" people how to be subjects of Empire.[4] If, in Bakhtin's terms, neoliberalism is, an authoritative discourse, a rhetoric that "cannot be questioned, [and] demand[s] and receive[s] unquestioned allegiance," then neoliberal pedagogy, likewise demands such allegiance that includes a logic of its own authority. As the first chapter will discuss, such a pedagogy is a "deliberately selective and connecting process which offers a historical and cultural ratification of a contemporary order." (qtd in Williams, *Marxism and Literature,* 116)

Neoliberalism, like other stages of capitalism, as an economic system has to be *written* into the social fabric in order to be given social meaning. We are not simply pointing to the discursive aspects of the economic, we are suggesting an expansion of the notion of writing such that we can see the economic as a product of intention, choice, and as crafted. We can begin to analyze the particular rhetorical strategies, if you will, of *writing* of neoliberal economic relation into the social fabric as an act of pedagogy. It's a process of approximating, normalizing, and writing, an established truth that has been posited discursively, rhetorically, and materially.

Against an authoritative discourse that demands allegiance, our purpose is to resituate pedagogy as a cultural practice that is capable of creating effective (and affective) responses and frameworks. We seek to offer situated examples of pedagogical strategies and practices that intervene in the dominant culture creating the possibilities of a democracy to come. In particular, we propose to move beyond a "theory/practice" divide that has marked debates concerning critical pedagogy. On one side of the divide are critical pedagogical theories that provide excellent analyses of the ideological and material implications of education and cultural practices, yet fall short when it comes to situated or local practice, opting instead for yet further calls for "what teachers *should* do." On the other side, are critical pedagogical practices that focus on the classroom as the primary, if not sole, site of pedagogy, eschewing broader theoretical implications of such practices and de-prioritizing non-classroom cultural spaces. By seeking to bridge this divide we hope to expand studies of pedagogy by considering pedagogy as a contingent, situated practice that brings theory and practice together and requires a language and orientation that reflects its particular cultural conjunction. With this purpose, this book, and books that follow it in the Lexington series Cultural Studies/Pedagogy/Activism, are directed towards expanding how we most broadly conceptualize pedagogy as lived political work. How can pedagogy be conceptualized so we see it as a site to intervene in culture and to act politically? How can we develop pedagogical strategies that work politically to make sense of and intervene in the world? How can we articulate the specific charge of pedagogy without collapsing it into cultural theory or limiting it to teaching techniques?

Our work on pedagogy engages with texts whose critique emerges from critical understanding of the current material conditions in which we live and whose purpose is to challenge dominant values and ideas. These materialist pedagogical texts such as work by Subcomandante Marcos, Michael Hardt and Antonio Negri, David Harvey, Chandra Mohanty, Raymond Williams, Gayatri Spivak, Jacques Derrida, Judith Butler, Susan Jarratt, and others, bring together pedagogy, theory, and democracy, particularly for those interested in writing and writing pedagogy, especially given recent calls for a return to the public spaces of democratic deliberation and participation. For example, Susan Wells has encouraged writing teachers to foreground public writing by considering the classroom as a version of the public sphere, analyzing public discourse, producing texts that enter into the public sphere, or writing at the intersections between the disciplines and the public (Wells 337–39). Pegeen Reichert Powell analyzes the public statements of the president of Miami University in response to a perceived hate crime on campus and the resulting two days of protest. Using Critical Discourse Analysis, she argues advocates for composition as a pedagogical space in which to "act[] against injustice in terms of our area of expertise: language and texts" (Powell 465). Nancy Fraser suggests that we attend to the cultural classifications and rhetorical labels that are "deployed to delegitimate some interests, views, and topics and to valorize others" (Fraser 131). The task of critical pedagogy, Fraser's work suggests, is to unpack how the rhetoric of economic privacy, for example, excludes particular issues from public debate. In particular, efforts to privatize economic issues and shield them from public debate have the effect of separating civil society from the state (Fraser 133). All of these scholars suggest that communicative practices are the site of pedagogical work and the site of democratic deliberation.

As we do this, we broaden the idea of schooling and education, arguing that "school" can or could be a site to remake the world. Educational spaces are in excess of classrooms: they are cultural locations outside of officially state sanctified sites. Part of the work of this book and of the series it introduces is to examine pedagogical sites, relationships, and possibilities that are in excess of the institution of the university or sites within the university that are in excess of its operations within neoliberalism.

While we do some of our pedagogical work within universities, we see these institutions as both places of possibility and places of limitation. Universities, on the one hand, train neoliberal workers; on the other hand, they are a site where young people make connections to communities that are beyond the walls of the university and in which they develop literacy practices that they use to communicate with and intervene in multiple publics. Our examples in this book move from the university into the world; they describe examples of critical literacies that connect students. In other books in the series, we discuss cultural sites of education that happen outside of authorized educational institutions.

In this framework, pedagogy has a complex purpose. It has a rhetorical interest in intervening in literate spaces in order to develop an understanding of new structures and in so doing develop a vocabulary for new, critical perspectives. This language is an integral part of political understandings of new and emergent structures and is fundamental to democratic participation. For example, Hardt and Negri argue that a theory of class not only gives us language in which to understand existing structures of class, it also gives us "potential lines" in which to understand class: "the task of a theory of class in this respect is to identify the existing conditions of potential collective struggle and express them as a political proposition" (Hardt and Negri 104). Pedagogy, as a contingent, situated practice that brings theory and practice together and requires a language and orientation that reflects its particular cultural conjunction, is necessarily engaged in a political practice of making, reproducing, and remaking language and social relations.

This articulation of pedagogy as situated practice that reflects the conjunctural moment is particularly important in the moment that we're in, what we've called neoliberalism. Hardt and Negri argue that in Empire communication is itself one of the key productive networks. Even the basic production of commodities in global sweatshops and tax-free "export-processing zones" has become more and more reliant upon communication networks, symbolic production, and the production and reproduction of social life—so that "the economic, the political, and the cultural increasingly overlap and invest one another" (xiii). Thus, the role of communication becomes central to establishing and maintaining Empire as well as resisting Empire—not at the level of ideology, but at the very heart of production. Understanding these networks of communication, including developing a critical language that can articulate the networks that overlap and invest each other, producing and reproducing social life, is fundamental pedagogical practice in the context of crises of globalization.

These articulations have a pedagogical force: they enable us to think about the historical and contemporary traditions of struggle that we can learn from so that our teaching—broadly conceived—can be immediately relevant to the literacy needs of agents of change. They give us ideas of how to struggle, how to act in local spaces that are touched by Empire, and how our communicative frameworks work against and through the forces of Empire. We ask: how can rhetoric "serve" democratic social movements? That is, if critical teachers are committed to deepening and expanding vocabularies for new, critical perspectives and for expanding democratic participation, what pedagogical strategies can help us understand the moment of globalization that we're in? How do we ask students to reframe their existing conceptual frameworks, asking them to walk different rhetorical pathways, and in so doing create a "new place" in the "non-place" of Empire? What does it mean to research and write in these spaces? How do we direct our pedagogical and political efforts towards Empire?

As the students, young people, and members of the community who participated in A-16 anti-globalization protests demonstrated, pedagogical praxis can be developed in a variety of cultural sites and by different social agents. Pedagogy, as A-16 demonstrated, is not solely the purview of institutionally trained professionals. Rather, pedagogy emerges from those who respond democratically to particular historical moments.

Notes

1. For readings that discuss the absence of discussions of pedagogy within the cultural studies tradition, see Eric J. Weiner, "Beyond 'Doing' Cultural Studies: Toward a Cultural Studies of Critical Pedagogy." Henry Giroux's work created conversations between traditions of critical theory and cultural studies. See the corpus of Giroux's work, most specifically, *Impure Acts* (Routledge: New York, 2000) and, most recently, "Resisting Market Fundamentalism and the New Authoritarianism: A New Task for Cultural Studies?" *JAC* 25.1 (2005).

2. For a review of the history of neoliberalism as a discourse and a policy, see David Harvey's *A Brief History of Neoliberalism*. Harvey's book is particularly good on the rhetoric of freedom in neoliberalism. For discussions of neoliberalism globally, and critical pedagogy, see Peter McLaren and Ramin Farahmandpur, "The Globalization of Capitalism and the New Imperialism: Notes Towards a Revolutionary Critical Pedagogy." For a discussion of neoliberalism in an American context, see Lisa Duggan, *Twilight of Equality*. For discussion of neoliberalism and women's labor, see Grace Chang, *Disposable Domestics: Immigrant Women Workers in the Global Economy*. For a discussion of neoliberalism and disability, see Robert Mcruer's, *Crip Theory: Cultural Signs of Queerness and Disability*. For a discussion of neoliberalism and the corporate university, see Chandra Mohanty's *Feminism Without Borders*, chapter six. Hardt and Negri discuss this as the expropriation of the commons.

3. Pierre Bourdieu argues that:

> neo-liberal discourse is not a discourse like others . . . it is a "strong discourse" which is so strong and so hard to fight because it has behind it all the powers of a world of power relations which it helps to make as it is, in particular by orienting the economic choices of those who dominate economic relations and so adding its own—specifically symbolic—force to those power relations. In the name of the scientific programme of knowledge, converted into a political programme of actions, an immense *political operation* is being pursued (denied, because it is apparently purely negative), aimed at creating the conditions for realizing and operating of the "theory"; a *programme of methodological destruction of collectives* (neo-classical economics recognizes only individuals, whether it is dealing with companies, trade unions, or families. (Bourdieu, *Acts*, 96)

Furthermore, as the market comes to dominate how we imagine what is possible—what are the boundaries within which we are policed, monitored, and allowed to exercise "democracy"—"public" space becomes subject to an ideological gentrification. Higher education, while far from being a bastion of democratic praxis, has nonetheless been one of the few remaining sites where oppositional knowledges and practices can be produced in a sustained way. Writing is but one site where the battle over the rules and boundaries of a post-Soviet era takes place. But it is an incredibly important one since writing is a site that preserves, reforms, and transforms how individuals and collectivities define what is possible.

4. In the fourth chapter, we will discuss neoliberal pedagogy in terms of Marx, Gayatri Spivak, and Stuart Hall's work on value where exchange value erases, or hides, the operations of cultural power.

Chapter 2
Articulating Action in a Neoliberal World

We have to decide whose side we're on and realize that our base of support has already been established by the very black and brown workers who clean our offices and to whom most of the faculty don't even speak. (Robbin Kelly, qtd in Kumar xxvi)

The move to connect education to the market has slowly eclipsed a parallel tradition of American higher education: to prepare students for their role as citizens in a democratic culture. In effect, the "crisis in the humanities" reflects a shift and struggle around the way in which literacies are valued. That is, if we are to understand that the primary role of education is to train students in specific literacy practices that shape, in part, how they see themselves as participants in the broader society and how they conceive of their relationship to labor, then a movement toward market-based literacies reflects a shift in values, and priorities, of higher education away from questions of democratic deliberation and participation to focus on the production of workers and consumers for the newest phase of the capitalist economy.

In this chapter, we analyze why and how these shifts and struggles have taken place, as well as provide a space to reconsider the ways in which, in the current conjuncture of neoliberalism, our higher education institutions contribute to, or limit, the kinds of literate practices necessary for expanding and deepening democratic traditions. As we discussed in the first chapter, rhetorical action does not represent simply a "new" framework for students and faculty to inject new energy into worn-out classroom practices. We would argue, instead, that rhetorical action seeks to open spaces for us to inquire into the social relations of capital that can be seen in conditions of education and in academic institutions. Further, we argue that we should understand rhetorical action as committed to spaces beyond the narrow confines of the classroom.

Our inquiry in this chapter includes an analysis of how and under what conditions knowledge is produced in educational institutions, opening up this discussion to analysis of labor, production, and consumption. In addition, we think that analyses of educational institutions need to account for more than the production of identities and ideologies. We consider how educational institutions are networked into communities through labor and their impact on local infrastructures (e.g. roads, waste, water use, public space). We link a discussion of labor to a discussion of democracy, arguing that discourses of labor shape how we see ourselves as participants in democratic society and how we imagine democracy itself. We then theorize the possibilities for agency, democratic participation, voice, feelings, and identity, in an era dominated by the alienation of knowledge and the avenues for effective participation, particularly knowledge about labor, and an educational force that encourages this alienation through market intersections and relations. These issues become increasingly important to address in a political climate that depends, in part, on advancing neoliberal market relations through rhetorics of fear, terror, and despair.

While we are concerned with the ways in which we can provide critical resources to critique these relations, we are also interested in how to open spaces to inquire into the social relations that education helps shape and questions about how we re-imagine practices capable of contextualizing education within larger educational and market forces. That is, we argue that the "creative" move, the "synthetic gesture" (Jarratt 24), component of a politically effective practice is essential in order to "establish the conditions for constructing socially functional, but always provisional, rhetorical [and political] speculations" (22, brackets ours). This process of establishing links and connections between the social relations of capital and the arena of education can lead to an intervention: generating practices and discourses that foreground the relationships between neoliberalism and labor gives us a space to articulate contradictions, differences, and possibilities that bring together differently situated groups.

This chapter asks what is unique and urgent about the conditions for higher education at our current conjuncture, and, just as importantly, asks what strategies, theories, languages and politics this moment requires. We seek to explore this new moment (or a moment, as we will discuss later, which is not new but an updated and restructured form of capitalism) and think through terms and practices that define it, examine why old strategies need to be reconceptualized (i.e. culturalist Marxist theories that drop an analysis of labor), and suggest practices and strategies of resistance. Our investment in reestablishing links between language, practices, and strategies of resistance, invites a consideration of useful intersections between cultural studies and critical rhetorical theory.

Neoliberalism as Public Pedagogy

Before we suggest how rhetorical action intervenes in struggles between practices that seek to deepen and expand democratic deliberation and participation, and those market-based literacies that seek to produce disciplined workers for the global market, it is useful to briefly discuss neoliberalism and why it is significant to our project. Broadly, neoliberalism is an economic policy of upward redistribution where social and political discourses provide a philosophy, a rhetorical framework, ideas about identity and citizenship that justify and explain privatization of public services, the opening of markets, and a lessening of government regulations on corporations. In short, neoliberalism extends market relations ever deeper into our social relations.[1] It can be described as the economic, political, and rhetorical practices of upward redistribution on a global scale and at the local level—a "greater concentration [of wealth and power] among fewer hands at the very top of an increasingly steep pyramid" (Duggan x). Neoliberalism, in one sense, is a way of defining work in relationship to culture that secures a workforce for capitalism. It is, in other words, a new historically produced social relation, a new way of mystifying and alienating labor as it creates an updated labor force for capital.

The process of establishing hegemony for neoliberalism requires more than simply changing the organization of the productive forces; it also requires "changes in the social use of language in work" (Choiliaraki and Fairclough 5). That is, neoliberal rhetorics are not merely discourses or ideologies. Rather, as Choliliarki and Fairclough argue, "economic, social, and cultural changes of late modernity . . . exist as *discourses* as well as processes that are taking place outside discourse, and . . . the processes that are taking place outside discourse are substantively shaped by these discourses" (94). In this sense, neoliberalism is a new world order that seeks to reconstruct social relations, economic structures, political institutions, and the form and content of our communication and social discourse. It is a vision of market as the arbiter of equality, as the *definitive* democratic form of social organization. It is a vision of politics as the arbiter of law and order that "protects" this market equality. And, it is a cultural consensus that creates (even as it mystifies) labor for production by separating the economic, the political, and the cultural. With David Harvey, we can see neoliberalism, as a new stage of capitalism (that is a social relationship) that constantly reconfigures itself to accommodate changing political and cultural conditions. As Harvey argues, neoliberalism "builds and rebuilds a geography in its own image. It constructs a distinctive geographical landscape, a produced space of transport and communications, of infrastructures and territorial organizations" (*A Brief History of Neoliberalism* 50).

Neoliberalism is a social relationship and is also a rhetoric: as Jarrattt argues, rhetorics are modes of personal, public, or private address that configure a relationship to power, that have their own internal logic, are connected to fixed forms and ideologies, and a dynamic history ("Beside Ourselves," 59). Rhetorics, we add to Jarratt, vis-à-vis Gayatri Spivak configure relationships to value. In *A Critique of Postcolonial Reason*, Spivak extends a reading of Derrida's notion of *différance* in which "all institutions of origin concealed the splitting off from something other than the origin, in order for the origin to be instituted" to a reading of capital (462). In her discussion of value, she shows how exchange value conceals the splitting off of use-value from exchange-value in order for value to be articulated into the logic of capital.[2] Spivak reads that which "must be deferred" by value in order for capitalism to establish itself (425). Therefore, when we use modes of address, we are connected to social relationships that produce relations to capital.

When we choose representations, following Jarratt, we make symbolic decisions that simultaneously figure relations of power and configure social relations, thus establishing a relationship to value. Representation, in the context of neoliberalism or any manifestation of capitalism, is not a neutral act. It is an act that activates social, political, cultural, and historical relationships of which we may not even be aware, that consolidates identities, and that interpellates bodies into systems of identity. It is also an act that creates everyday affective responses and habits, and that creates relationships across public and private spheres. Insofar as representation is an act, it is a rhetoric—that is, it is an interested discursive act that intervenes in a particular conjuncture and affects that conjuncture. Neoliberal rhetoric is intended to preserve, stabilize, and extend capitalist social/labor-relations, with the particular purpose of producing laboring subjects.

As a rhetoric, as a world vision, as a system of value, as relationship between labor and capital, as a politics, and as a cultural consensus, neoliberalism is also a pedagogy: a mode of education that exists in a variety of cultural sites that incorporates subjects into dominant neoliberal ideology. To rewrite Bourdieu's notion of neoliberalism as a "strong rhetoric" (*Acts*, 96), neoliberalism is a "strong" and persuasive pedagogy that is embedded in the particular relations between State and capitalist power. Neoliberalism, in other words, becomes an educational force of culture that shapes how we are literate, how literacy is defined, and who is literate because of its constitutive relationship to labor. As it prepares students to enter the workforce, either as skilled or unskilled laborers, neoliberal pedagogy interpellates subjects into relationships between labor and capital. And more, it interpellates subjects into *social relations* that support the circulation and realization of capital in our daily lives. That is, neoliberal pedagogy is not interested solely in producing specific laboring subjects for the *workplace;* it seeks to produce subjects whose lives are fully subsumed within the logic of the global market. Neoliberalism is therefore a pedagogy produced in a variety of public spaces, social sites, in civil society, as well as in traditional educational locations. Neoliberalism, as Henry Giroux argues:

> marks the space of a new kind of public pedagogy, one in which the production, dissemination, and circulation of ideas emerges from the educational force of the larger culture. Public pedagogy in this sense refers to a powerful ensemble of ideological and institutional forces whose aim is to produce competitive, self-interested individuals vying for their own material and ideological gain…Corporate public pedagogy has become an all-encompassing cultural horizon for producing market identities, values and practices. (74)

As neoliberalism configures relationships of power and between labor and capital, consolidates identities, interpellates bodies into systems of identity, and creates relationships across public and private spheres, it creates deep and even violent economic, political, and cultural ruptures. As Robert Mcruer argues, neoliberalism forces the poor and those designated as minorities (those who the Zapatistas describe as "the indigenous, youth, women, homosexuals, lesbians, people of color, immigrants, workers, peasants; the majority who make up the world basements") to "accommodate" to this new world order.[3] Those who fall outside of the dominant ideological and labor system—disabled, women, children, ethnic groups, as a few examples—must fall outside the protections of civil society. As the Zapatistas of Mexico have famously argued, neoliberalism is an "international economic order that has already caused more death and destruction than the great world wars." (264)

In the context of education, those who want to challenge the rhetorical, economic, political, and social hegemony of neoliberalism need to articulate the systems of representation that activate pedagogical, political, cultural, and historical relationships in ways that concretely pose alternatives. Our practices, educational strategies, activist work and theories are directed towards intervention in the different sites in which neoliberalism produces public pedagogy. We therefore argue that the context of education includes more than the classroom. Rather, our identities and literacies are formed through complex cultural educational systems that include media, social practices, and state apparatuses that constitute the rhetorics and practices of maintaining hegemony. While educational institutions are important sites of intervention, we believe that for action to be effective, it is crucial that we consider the educational networks that are both challenged and reinforced within the university. That is, we want to think through how our actions can be interventions into the web of educational networks that cultivate and reproduce neoliberal social relations.

In his well-known introduction to *Keywords*, Raymond Williams argues that words themselves are a crucial area of cultural intervention. If we see language as something that we use to actively shape, make, challenge, change our society, as Williams suggests, we can open up space for social change. We *do* things through and with rhetoric: rhetoric motivates people to take action, sets up boundaries of inclusion (and exclusion), establishes who is allowed to speak, who belongs to a community, whose work is valued, whose work can be spoken about, etc. (Powell 442). As Williams argues, a focus on rhetoric enables us to explore:

> crucial area of social and cultural discussion, which has been inherited within precise historical and social conditions and which has to be made at once conscious and critical—subject to change as well as to continuity—if the millions of people in whom it is active are to see it as active: not a tradition to be learned, nor a consensus to be accepted, nor a set of meanings which, because it is "our language", has a natural authority; but as a shap-

ing and reshaping, in real circumstances and from profoundly different
and important points of view: a vocabulary to use, to find our own ways in,
to change as we find it necessary to change it, as we go on making our
own language and history. (24–25)

While Williams draws our attention to the crucial role of language and discourse
in political struggle, we can extend his analysis a bit further. That is, rhetoric is
at the intersection of analysis and action insofar as it requires us to carefully
analyze the particular conjuncture of events, discourses, interests, habits, and
values of a particular exigency in order to discern effective courses of action.
Rhetorical theory is most often understood as being concerned primarily with
linguistic intervention. However if we are to take seriously Hardt and Negri's
argument that the logic of Empire, what we have been calling neoliberalism,
channels relations of control and rule ever more into the "communicative machine" (32) and that neoliberal capitalism extends into the "production and reproduction of life itself" (24), then the historical association between rhetoric
and the political/linguistic sphere seems a bit suspect. Put another way, rhetorics
of rule and resistance, cannot simply be thought of in terms of *language* as a
separate and distinct sphere. Interventions and disruptions of neoliberalism need
to take a broader view of persuasion and rhetorical action.

For example, if we argue along with David Harvey's interpretation of
Marx that capital seeks to appropriate labor and to reproduce the social relations
necessary to bring capital into the world, then when we participate in rhetoric
that is "intended to work persuasively in particular cultural situations," we participate in social relations that are intended to create capital. Neoliberal rhetorics,
then, are persuasive not simply at the level of ideology (as separate and distinct
from a material base). They are persuasive in the material ways in which they
craft and direct our very "modes of life" (Marx, *German Ideology*, 42), on our
bodies, identities, and emotions. Such rhetorics function to configure relationships to labor, production, and consumption. When we write and produce culture,
we configure a relationship to labor and therefore to capital.

As we'll discuss in the subsequent chapter, rhetorics produce bodily affects and shape identities and emotions. Rhetoric activates social, political, cultural, and historical relationships that we may not even be aware of; consolidates
identities; interpellates bodies into systems of identity; and creates relationships
across public and private spheres. These rhetorics are intended to preserve, stabilize, and extend capitalist labor-relations, with the particular purpose of creating and maintaining workers as appendages of capital. And to create and maintain workers in such a relationship to capital within neoliberalism, requires *material persuasion* through "bio-political production" (Hardt and Negri 24), or
what we are calling, neoliberal rhetorics.

Williams's work also suggests that rhetoric can be the site to disrupt
and transform these social relations. When dominant discourses are naturalized
as common sense, seen as part of an inherited tradition, or part of some universal
truth, critical literacy lies in understanding that rhetoric—the ideas and concepts

that it embodies as well as words that are used to articulate these ideas and concepts—are not natural or traditional but discourses that we use to create our own culture and our own meaning. David Harvey, reading Gramsci on critical inquiry, argues that the task for critical inquiry is "to penetrate to the underlying meaning of such phenomena and to explore their ramifications for daily life." We're expanding on this notion of critical inquiry in our discussion of Williams through our emphasis on rhetoric—in this moment, the languages of everyday life through which we make our world – and our emphasis on effective courses of action (*Spaces of Global Capitalism*, 83). A critical rhetorical approach goes beyond merely "understanding" the social production of common sense—it turns our attention to praxis. Some recent work in rhetorical theory has made moves in this direction, or at least in a direction that speaks to our present concerns. In his reappropriation of the ancient Sophist Gorgias's practice of *kairos*—a "certain confluence of utterance and time, or to a marking of time with speech" (Poulakos 89)—John Poulakos argues that the rhetor does not simply craft her rhetoric to suit existing contexts or, conversely, wait until the "appropriate moment" to have her intervention be intelligible. Rather, "rhetorical action" can target "any established belief" by creating "room for new beliefs by reference to additional principles" that are also present in a culture at any given historical moment (95).

In our final chapter, we'll discuss Zapatista writing and rhetoric which represents such a revolutionary break from neoliberal discourse and hegemony. This break is at once rhetorical and political, but it is about bringing them together—rhetorical action as political action/political action as rhetorical. In this sense, Zapatista writing is *kairotic*. Poulakos sees Gorgias's notion of *kairos* as having a three-fold lesson for rhetors:

> First, any established belief, be it scientific, logical, or philosophical, constitutes an opportunity for rhetorical action. Depending on the orator's ingenuity, artistry, and swiftness of thought, rhetorical action ought to aim at the production of new arguments . . . Second, the orator must create room for new beliefs by reference to additional principles (i.e., human action is also a function of circumstances greater than human will) . . .Third, the orator must construe the audience addressed as susceptible to and welcoming of artistic innovation...When all three of these suggestions are followed, the orator toils to revisit a familiar discursive terrain and resettle it in more attractive ways. By doing so, the orator can be said to subject a fixed belief to the power of *kairos*, which "takes the same things and makes them disgraceful and then alters them and makes them seemly." (95)

To rewrite Poulakos's rethinking of Gorgias's concept of *kairos*, we can see rhetorical action as three-fold. First, rhetorical actions should aim at the production of new critical literacies. This depends in part upon the rhetor's "ingenuity, artistry and swiftness of thought," yes, but also that rhetor's relationship to power and ability to create relationships in conjunction with dominant, emergent, and pre-emergent structures of feeling. Second, the rhetor creates an openness for new practices and affective relationships that are already existing, but not yet articulated in a recognizable, strategic, or liberatory form. Third, Poulakos suggests that the "rhetor must construe the audience as susceptible to and welcoming of, artistic innovation" (94). We would reconstrue his use of "susceptible"—conjuring up images of "duping" your audience—to mean openness to structures of feeling bonds, intersubjectivity, as well as an "openness to many works of art" (Williams 114).

So when all of these three suggestions are followed, the rhetor can disrupt or rupture a familiar, or dominant, discursive terrain in order to create a "certain openness and unknowingness" (Butler 39). While Poulakos focuses on resettling things in a more "attractive" way, we would emphasize "becoming part of a process the outcomes of which no one subject can surely predict" (39). That is, we emphasize not positing, or predetermining, a "truth" or something that is *a priori* known, but suggesting something that cannot yet be seen, something unarticulated, something that is to come and that can only be made within the interstitial spaces of collective affective bonds. Put another way, rhetorical action may not respond in ways that are recognizably rhetorical—where "rhetorical" is understood as a linguistic construction, a counter-argument. Rather, rhetorical action might respond by opening up connections among subjects that make possible solidarity. However, this solidarity does not have a predetermined shape or familiarity—it must be made with and among those subjects. We will discuss such a move in chapter 5 when we look at the discursive and emotional moments of a persuasive cultural argument of neoliberalism.

This notion of rhetoric gets us away from reliance upon belief, or an established universal truth, or settled narrative, to the kind of openness to the democracy that Butler, Derrida, and the Zapatistas are talking about: a response to the current moment that calls into question not what we know but *how we know what we know* in order to become something and someone(s) different. Words and writing for the Zapatistas are an active means of making the world, the activity of language is a means of creating cultural and political meaning. When they began their insurrection in 1994, Marcos famously declared in a communiqué that described the contributions of women to the Zapatista movement that "The war for the word has begun" (7).

Rhetoric as difference, divergence from authority and as productive, opens up rhetoric to discussions of democracy. Zapatista rhetoric, as it is open to difference and as it actively creates political possibilities, aims to produce new literacies. When we think of rhetoric as speaking and acting not just against hegemony but beyond hegemony, our work is political: it excavates and intervenes in received systems of meaning. This notion of rhetoric, as Paul de Man argues, "puts into question a whole series of concepts that underlie the value judgments of our critical discourse" (16). James Clifford observes in the context of a discussion of culture, that language as public participation and action is "less about how to speak well than about how to speak at all, and to act meaningfully, in the world of public cultural symbols" (*Writing Culture*, 11).

Susan Jarratt argues that the political charge of rhetoric—that is the charge of rhetorical action—in the traditions emphasized by Poulakos, entails a "strong obligation to action in the social and pedagogical world" (Jarratt, *Re-reading*, 24). Such an orientation to action has been hampered, she argues, by the academic left's preoccupation with poststructuralism insofar as it has emphasized a practice of critique and undecidability, leaving "no room for political struggle" (68).[4] In subsequent chapters, our interest in opening up rhetoric into rhetorical action reflects our orientation for political struggle.

Rhetorical action for political struggle—in a cultural Marxist tradition—lies in literacy: the ways in which we use language and discourse more generally to shape our society and the ways in which languages and discourses shape us. In this vein, Angela Hewett and Robert Mcruer argue that the task of critical analysis lies in "interrogating how such discourses function as a rhetoric—that is, as nonnatural, constructed discourses intended to work persuasively in particular cultural situation" (103). Rhetoric, as Derrida's work suggests, is not merely a function of capitalism but is mobilized by those who want to change the social relations that capital seeks to create and maintain. And this is part of the historic charge of rhetoric—not merely to critique (i.e. through the dialectic) but to determine the most effective modes of intervention—the "available means" to borrow from Aristotle—and effect action within a specific conjunctural moment. That is, we see critical traditions of rhetoric as helping provide a language for thinking about a two-fold charge in the specific context of neoliberalism: first, to critically analyze and critique neoliberal social relations and pedagogical strategies used to reproduce them; and, second, to develop effective strategies for creating exigencies within the current hegemony within which our interventions can be contingently effective. We, then, conceive of rhetorical action as being concerned with both critique and the creative work of producing discursive interventions. That is, it is not enough to critique the rhetorics of neoliberalism; it is as important to consider the most effective ways to intervene, disrupt, and construct alternatives to neoliberalism.

In Oskar Negt and Alexander Kluge's text, *Public Sphere and Experience: Toward an Analysis of the Bourgeois and Proletarian Public Sphere*, they offer several important considerations for rhetorical action in a neoliberal context. They argue that the very organization and discursive construction of the hegemonic public sphere limits the capacity for effective intervention when we participate on its terms. Further, by consenting to participate within the terms of the dominant public, we can actually be complicit in *maintaining* it:

> as soon as the worker participates in the bourgeois public sphere, once he [sic] has won elections, taken up union initiatives, he is confronted by a dilemma. He can make only "private" use of a public sphere that has disintegrated into a mere intermediatry sphere. The public sphere operates according to this rule of private use, not according to the rules whereby the experiences and class interests of workers are organized. The interests of workers appear in the bourgeois public sphere as nothing more than a gi-

gantic, cumulative "private interest," not as a collective mode of production for qualitatively new forms of public sphere and public consciousness. To the extent that the interests of the working class are no longer formulated and represented as genuine and autonomous vis-à-vis the bourgeois public sphere, betrayal by individual representatives of the labor movement ceases to be an individual problem . . . In wanting to use the mechanisms of the bourgeois public sphere for their cause, such representatives become, objectively, traitors to the cause they are representing. (7)

The "private" nature of the public sphere's communicative organization draws our attention to one aspect of material persuasion—an aspect that is important to our interest in rhetorical action. We need to be attentive to the rhetorical construction of the conditions of communication and public engagement. Negt and Kluge suggest that under the dominant communicative organization even the best articulations, best in the sense that they are representative of the interests of the working class or other social movements, are *necessarily* articulated within the public sphere as individual articulations, or collections of individual articulations, leaving the dominant logic of the public sphere intact. Collective experience is *unthinkable* within the communicative context of the dominant public sphere. What is more, any notion of a singular collective subjectivity is a fiction; the collective experiences of the working classes cannot be reduced to a singular unity (44). Working class experience is marked by its specificity, differentiation, and localized contextualization (43). In other words, entering the dominant public means being caught between two inadequate modes of representation: a collection of individuals or as a fictive collectivity.

Negt and Kluge argue that counter-hegemonic struggle needs to have a constructive, creative, and alternative orientation in relation to the dominant public sphere. They argue that, the "only antidotes to the production of the illusory public sphere are the counter-products of a proletarian public sphere: idea against idea, product against product, production sector against production sector" (79–80). That is, we are arguing for the need to articulate contingent interventions into neoliberalism that critique its rhetorics, create openings and/or disruptions, and creatively exercise our capacity to construct alternatives. We have no illusions that offering up counter-productions will, by itself, fundamentally transform neoliberalism. Rather, such counter-productions work to build an alternative articulation of social relations *over time*.

From our position, then, this work with rhetoric entails more than interpretation. If we just work at the level of interpretation, as Harry Cleaver argues, our work is limited to academic discussions and academic audiences. Interpretations of capital that are just interpretations ignore the political implications of the rhetoric: its role in constituting the social relations of capital. Rhetorical analysis must, therefore, include discussion of the political applications and objectives of rhetoric: rhetorical analysis in the interests of social change, including *re-articulation* of labor. Such work must "eschew all detached interpretation and abstract theorizing in favor of grasping concepts only within that concrete totality of struggle whose determinations they designate" (Cleaver 11). Our objective is to disrupt rhetorics that organize social relations of capital and create strategic interventions in the interest of social change. As we will argue later, strategic rhetorics seeking to re-articulate social relations are complex insofar as they do not seek to simply posit an alternative, utopian or "better" future. Rather, they require a re-articulation of the whole complex of social relations—productive and reproductive labor, structures of feeling, identities, agency, voice, and democratic participation. Yet, we also recognize that such re-articulations can only be local/contingent (that is a response to a specific conjuncture) as long as capitalist material relations remain intact.

As this opening of Williams's discussion of rhetoric into a discussion of the social relations of capital suggests, we can see the social relations that produce workers as appendages of capital and rhetoric as a mode in which to develop an active conscious and critical relationship to labor. Labor, first of all, is more than something we do when we're at a job. Labor involves the labor process—all the social relations, rhetorics, feelings, identifications, ideologies that are mobilized to create capital. Reconfiguration of labor, for example, includes, as feminist critics have recognized, the division capitalism has created between productive (labor in the factory) and reproductive (labor in the home) and all the social relations that support this division.

Academic Institutions

Academic institutions are not "mere sites of instruction" but spaces in which formal processes of socialization occur within the context of capitalist social relations (Hewett and Mcruer, Mohanty, Williams). Hewett and Mcruer argue that administrators, faculty and students "constitute [universities] as 'points of production'—reproducing the social relations necessary . . . to bring capital into the world" (97). Danika Brown argues futher that universities are institutions in which dominant, class-based interests are consolidated. This consolidation often gives the appearance of inclusion, change, and progress, as critics of diversity and multiculturalism have argued (Powell, Mahoney). But rather than progressive change, universities are spaces in which calls for change can be folded back into hegemony. Traditions of protest and containment can serve to both produce and protect hegemony. Brown argues:

> Higher education in America plays a significant role in defining social relations under a dominant socioeconomic system in several ways: by transmitting the cultural values of that system and by producing technologies and skilled workers for that system. In addition, the institution of higher education is a significant site for containment of resistance to the dominant system. Higher education is a social institution understood as having the resources and expertise necessary for identifying and providing solutions to social problems; however, those problems and solutions are

most often defined in terms of the interests of the dominant system that created the institution. At the same time, institutions of higher education are also constructed as somehow separate from larger society. For example, discourses of the differences between university life and the "real world" are pervasive and campuses are large contained geographies: thus, the protest and resistance on university campuses has been generally tolerated and expected. (Brown 321)[5]

Brown's work suggests that traditions of protest and discursive challenges to the status quo appear to offer spaces of contestation. However, as Rosemary Hennessy's work suggests, while universities are often thought of as bastions of liberal thought, they are caught up in "waves" of neoliberal economic policies, ideologies and pedagogies: "tuition at state colleges and universities and the tenure system have been two targets of economic policies, the growth of part-time faculty and a pervasive 'corporatizing' being two of its most glaring symptoms" (41). As a result, there has been much pressure to reshape curriculum, policies, rhetoric, and relations with students (among other things) more closely to the demands and goals of the neoliberal marketplace. These attempts to reshape the educational process in universities are integrally connected to the labor conditions of teachers and the ways in which "education" and "teachers" are constructed in the broader public. That is, neoliberal pedagogies work to reshape processes of education and labor at the same time as they reconstruct our language and affective relationships to education and educational workers.

In this context of neoliberalism where there is pressure to shape education to goals of the neoliberal marketplace, universities become spaces of accommodation, consolidation of power, reification of relationship between capital and labor, and preservation of the status quo. In her discussion of fields such as women's studies, black studies, and ethnic studies, Chandra Mohanty argues that these areas represent spaces of oppositional knowledge that run the risk of accommodation and de-politization in the academy. For example, universities can claim to be free and open spaces that are tolerant of ideas and identities historically excluded from public and university spaces by having centers of research that focus on minority issues and populations or that have organizations that support members of these populations (e.g. Multicultural Student Centers, Lesbian/Gay/Bi Student groups, Hispanic Student Groups, Commissions on the Status of Women, Diversity Training Workshops). However, at the same time that universities support these departments and organizations, they underpay workers from minority populations or contract out positions to keep them low wage. One only needs take a walk across campus from the Multicultural Center to the dining hall to see the glaring disconnect between institutional support for underrepresented groups and the ways in which labor relations materially reinforce neoliberal social relations. The creation of these academic fields can, in effect, mystify relationships between capital and labor as long as the separation between the "educational process" and labor is maintained.

We also want to foreground another gap in the way the problem of academic institutions is posed. Further buttressing the "separate status" of the university, the university itself is a model, a training ground if you will, for class formation, reproduction, and consciousness. Both ideologically and materially, universities model the split between mental and manual labor inside the institution itself. For example, food service workers are somehow "outside" the "work" of the university. The often touted "university community" is an imagined community of students, faculty, and academic administrators engaged in the project of "education." Service workers (food service, custodial, grounds, etc.) are constructed to be both inside and outside the university at the same time. They are "inside" insofar as they reproduce the conditions of "education" for the "university community;" they are outside insofar as they are not imagined as part of the community itself. This separation between mental and manual work is further sharpened as universities increase their reliance on contracted labor. Service workers "work" in the space of the university, but their labor is paid for by an outside corporation. With contracting reproductive labor comes a contracting out of "community responsibility," resigning essential service and reproductive labor employees to a kind of H-2B worker status in the "educational community."

Furthermore, academic institutions are not merely sites in which knowledge and students are produced. These institutions produce much more than these readily recognizable features of higher education. Academic institutions produce food, clean spaces for living, waste products, garbage, and jobs in a range of service industries devoted to reproductive labor. They also produce patterns of commuting, discourses of achievement and success, and relations with corporate and State institutions. That is, if we view academic institutions as a whole, not only through their stated educational missions, we have a much more accurate and inclusive picture of these institutions through the social relations they establish, construct, and maintain within a broader social division of labor. That is, part of what analysis necessitates is an understanding of academic institutions not *merely* as educational institutions. They are complex social institutions that encompass the range of social and labor relations of neoliberal capitalist relations.

Rhetorical Action

In the first chapter, we argued that our objectives are to explore "a curiosity that is critical, bold, and adventurous," and in so doing develop new critical understandings. We argued that this is a cultural practice that is capable of creating effective responses to the conjectural moment. Rhetorical action, in this sense, has an interest in intervening in literate spaces in order to determine the most effective modes of intervention, to effect action within a specific conjunctural moment, and to develop vocabularies for practice.

If universities are contradictory spaces—spaces where different ideas and exigencies converge, where opportunities for democratic practice are both created and foreclosed—what are the possibilities for rhetorical action in these fraught contexts? In other words, what are the practices that produce new articulations and in so doing set the stage for agency and democratic participation? To put it another way, what are the rhetorical strategies that respond to the moment and can be meaningful within these circumstances?

In *Prison Notebooks*, Gramsci provides a discussion of how, from within educational sites that are hegemonic, we can become attentive to the multiple and conflictual meanings of language, reading against and beyond the authoritative rhetorics of neoliberal pedagogy, and using this reading to open up critical possibilities. In his discussion on education, Gramsci describes how state-run education tries to indoctrinate students in its own beliefs. The state does this by teaching students the study of grammar of Latin and Greek that is intended to teach discipline, obedience, and precision: it is a method of pedagogic indoctrination that schools students in the interests of the state.

From reading different languages, however, the student becomes familiar with an entire linguistic and cultural process that does not involve the authority of the state. Within the rhetoric of the Latin and Greek writers students read *differences* between historical periods and among authors. Through this reading, students "discover the grammar and the vocabulary of Phaedrus are not those of Cicero, nor those of Plautus, nor of Lactantius or Tertullian, and that the same nexus of sounds does not have the same meaning in different periods for different authors" (Gramsci 39). Moreover, as the student compares the differences between Latin and Italian, she realizes that each word takes on different meanings according to the period and the writer in each language under consideration. These differences suggest the play of rhetoric in a Bakhtinian and Derridian tradition: where "all institutions of origin concealed the splitting off from something other than the origin, in order for the origin to be instituted."[6] Students undertake a critical reading of that which "must be deferred" in order for an authoritative rhetoric to establish itself (Spivak, *A Critique of Postcolonial Reason*, 425).

Gramsci says that from the study of Latin and Greek, a student can read "the distinction and the identification of words and concepts; [these words and concepts] suggest the whole of formal logic, from the *contradiction* between opposites to the analysis of distincts; reveals the historical movement of the entire language, modified through time, developing and not static" (38, our italics). Gramsci suggests that reading contradiction, bringing together things that don't make sense. However, generally this "bringing together" works in the interest of power. For Gramsci, however, this act of reading is more than simply reading contradictions of power. Such an attentive student is "capable of the highest degrees of specialization" despite the fact that she might come from a social group "which has not traditionally developed the appropriate attitudes" (38). She can read between languages, both within contemporary Italian as well as in historical and cultural times and with different authors, the work of difference. In so doing, students open up language to the work of différance, noting the influences and authority that work and are worked through in rhetoric.

These moments of reading, when students pass through the various stages of rhetoric, allow the student to develop a historicized understanding of differences expressed through the ways in which rhetoric is used, persuasively and strategically, and even in the interest of creating opportunities for democratic action.[7] This is, in part, a practice of reading power. As the student becomes altered to the complexity of these rhetorics and engages in them, she reads vastly different state interests and class positions. These moments of reading allow students to see powerful interests that are invested in language. Differences in the way rhetoric is understood allow her to read and distinguish different class interests and state interests. Thus, reading takes place despite the fact that the student is reading from within an educational system that seeks to perpetuate hegemonic interests. But, as Gramsci suggests, the student is doing more than reading *against* power: she is reading possibilities for uncovering structures of the text and reading for possible meaning. Gramsci calls this critical capacity "good sense":

> Each one of us changes himself, modifies himself to the extent that he changes and modifies the complex relations of which he is the hub. In this sense the real philosopher is and cannot be other than, the politician, the active man who modifies the environment, understanding by environment the ensemble of relations which each of us enters to take part in. If one's own individuality is the ensemble of those relations, to create one's personality means to acquire consciousness of them and modify ones own personality means to modify the *ensemble* of these relations. (qtd. in Harvey, *Spaces of Global Capitalism*, 84)

This is precisely what we take Victor Villanueva to mean when he argues that "[r]hetoric, after all, is how ideologies are carried, how hegemonies are maintained. Rhetoric, then, would be the means by which hegemonies could be countered" (Villanueva 121).

Gramsci's work on academic institutions suggests that they can be spaces for the proliferation of neoliberal pedagogy and accommodation of social resistance, and at the same time there are institutional traditions and rhetorics that exceed the boundaries of authoritative rhetorics. Our objective in this final section is to identify areas of reading difference, and argue that reading difference serves as an opening into rhetorical action that will serve as an opening for a more extensive discussion of these strategies. Because we see educative relationships in the larger context of culture, our examples come from both inside and outside the classroom.

As our experiences both as teachers and as activists have demonstrated, activism is circumscribed by the conflict between the university's neoliberal ideology that values the production of finished, marketable writing and a cultural studies tradition that values writing as a space to develop agency, voice, and history.

The struggle between neoliberalism—as a practice and ideology that transforms political and cultural values as economic ones—and cultural studies—anti-disciplinary, activist practice that is aligned with anti-capitalist critique—creates contingent circumstances that students and faculty must negotiate. Our inquiry in this project is situated in a cultural studies tradition that recognizes and examines the "very powerful pressures" which are "expressed in political, economic, and cultural formations" (Williams, *Marxism and Literature,* 87) and uses this critical work to develop strategies for re-articulating, even re-imagining, economic and cultural imperatives of neoliberalism. Our discussion of sites of intervention, therefore, must acknowledge the tensions, contradictions, and contingencies that are produced in the conflict between neoliberal pedagogy and rhetorical action and acknowledge the foreclosures of class alliance that these tensions and contradictions produce. These pressures can be seen as pedagogical, what Giroux calls an educational force of the larger culture, in the sense that they seek to define, instruct, or even discipline us in the possibilities for social life, public ideas, and identity formations.

The fact that activism needs to negotiate a wide range of powerful pressures (institutional, social, discursive, and cultural) at any particular moment, underscores the rhetorical component of such pedagogies. While critical analysis of neoliberal pedagogies seeks to map the continuity and systemic nature of the current hegemony, rhetorical action opens up pedagogy to a concern with identifying and creating *dis*continuities within neoliberalism. As Gerard Hauser suggests, "the need for discourse arises most pointedly at times when disruptions or gaps occur in the normal course of events"—we would add, when political action *creates* such disruptions or gaps (Hauser 6). These disruptions rarely happen on a systemic scale. They usually are situated within specific institutional and local contexts. The "non-rhetorical elements that are part of the complex forces in which communication occur . . . serve as opportunities or limitations" for rhetorical action (8). Rhetorical action, is, then "situated action" rooted in contingency with a goal of using "symbols to induce social action" (3). We do not intend to dismiss or displace critical analysis and focus solely on the pragmatics of a given situation. Rather, we argue that *both* are necessary for struggles against neoliberal capitalism that seek to cultivate alternatives.

We see the classroom as one space in which educational relationships are built and engaged. However, as Williams suggests, educational relationships exist within culture generally and the dominant system finances and distributes knowledge in a variety of cultural sites:

> with what the whole environment, its institutions and relationships, actively and profoundly teaches. To consider the problems of families, or of town planning, is then an educational enterprise, for these, also, are where teaching occurs . . . For who can doubt, looking at television or newspapers, or reading the women's magazines, that here, centrally, is teaching, and teaching financed and distributed in a much larger way than is formal education? (*Communications,* 15)

It is for this reason that rhetorical action must confront neoliberalism on multiple cultural levels: in classrooms, in residence halls, on university websites, in official university documents and communications, on talk shows, in the community, and in the streets, to achieve consent.

Working with communities both inside and outside the classroom, our work begins with a cultural studies model seeking to transform educational relationships from spaces/identities and practices that reproduce and instruct in neoliberal interests to spaces that critique the status quo and, even, provide a vision of counter-hegemony. We draw from a variety of critical traditions (queer, feminist, Zapatista, Freirian, to name a few) that resist monologic, disciplining meanings of pedagogy. We insist upon a multiplicity of critical approaches not in the sense of traditional notions of pluralism. Rather, we recognize that neoliberalism is *particularlized* in any given social/insitutional space. As Guattari and Negri have argued, the task of new forms of radical political organization is to reject doctrinal or programmatic forms of political organization. Instead these new forms of radical political organization are "concerned with a plurality of relations within a multiplicity of singularities" that make possible "articulating the different dimensions of social intellection" and "neutralizing the destructive power of capitalist arrangements" (Guattari and Negri 107). We emphasize dialogic language: a materialist theory of knowledge in the form of cultural texts and the use of language, writing, and symbols as a form of social action and agency. As a result, we advocate strategies of writing, thinking, and working that create us as agents and provide us with entrance into communities as activists and intellectuals. This work identity enables us to rethink our relationships to labor and rethink identities that are produced by existing labor relations. These strategies produce counter-hegemonic knowledge and spaces, allowing us to re-imagine the world that we live in and develop capacities to act.

Overview

The process of becoming aware of how language figures in the production, maintenance, and contestation of hegemonies both requires work and enables future production of language and society. Becoming attentive to how language shapes and is shaped by our world is a mode of agency where language users, writers, students, faculty, cultural workers, activists, and others can create the material conditions in which they live. In fact, forging language to carry meaning that produces our material and social lives can enable us to build new educative relationships, to create our own history, and even, if sometimes only temporarily, public spaces and institutions which realize our values and ambitions. This approach draws from Williams's argument that social meaning is created in and through language in social groups. For example, Rachel uses the language from *Keywords* in a class encouraging students to become aware of how we use language and become aware of how language is linked to structures of dominance. This move asks students to attend to how language shapes and is shaped by our world and how language is a mode of agency where language users, writers, students, faculty, cultural workers, activists, and others can create the material conditions in which we live. In fact, students are encouraged to develop writing projects that are linked to communities and activist work.

As student writers use language as a mode of agency, as they experience how it can be used to build new educative relationships and recreate the material conditions in which they live, a cultural studies pedagogy serves as an entrance into communities as activists and intellectuals. To echo Williams's language, as we make the historical conditions in which we live both conscious and critical, we can begin to create new spaces, new publics, to imagine new identities, and can forge new communities. Such spaces "contest . . . the exclusionary norms of the bourgeois public, elaborating alternative styles of political behavior and alternative norms of public speech" (Williams, *Marxism and Literature*, 116).

In publicly presenting his work at a public lecture series, one student discovered how writing can serve as a commitment to a subordinated discourse community and a contribution to its cultural politics. Jason Hipp's paper written on gay identity situates writing as a space to acknowledge and perhaps transform the complex ways in which communities are organized. His presentation served as an entrance into the community as an activist and intellectual, and opened up spaces of communication at the same time as it contested dominant visions of gay identity. In particular, Jason offered the LBGT community a critique of the discourse on marriage, one intended to reconstitute its vision of itself on its own terms. In so doing, Jason's essay offered his audience ways to revision the public spaces they inhabit, perhaps even ways to reconfigure mainstream notions of identity.

In Kevin's Advanced Composition course, "Global Literacies," students examined intersections among transnational capitalism, consumer identities, the language of the market, and the possibilities for citizen participation. Students were routinely outraged by the exploitative relations created by neoliberal, global capitalism and its impact upon local communities both in the US and abroad. Their outrage has additional significance given their personal histories growing up in the coal and steel producing regions in Eastern Pennsylvania—a region that has seen mass plant closures as the result of global competition. However, their outrage frequently turns to despair or cynicism because they do not see effective possibilities for change. Over the course of a semester, they inquired into the common cultural arguments that mediate between their outrage and their cynicism. That is, as a class they began to identify and reconstruct common neoliberal rhetorics that contain their outrage through discourses of cynicism, hopelessness, and despair. Such an inquiry often led to discussions of the material constraints on political participation, educational goals, and identities.

One of the neoliberal argumentative strategies most often articulated by Kevin's Advanced Composition students mirrors Fukuyama's "end of history" thesis and Margaret Thatcher's famous proclamation that "there is no alternative." This argumentative strategy enables students (and individuals more broadly) to maintain a sense of themselves as "good people" by allowing them to recognize injustice and acknowledge their own moral commitments, while suppressing action because of the seeming impossibility of any other option. Students thus internalize a complex argumentative structure that reproduces neoliberal social relations (because that argument denies imagining concrete avenues for change), but also produces affective "traces"—that is, students are left feeling cynical or despairing. Once the class generated these rhetorical strategies, they resituated these strategies as a problem. That is, how can they disrupt the strategy in order to avoid despair or cynicism as an inevitable conclusion—and by extension, their complicity in reproducing neoliberal social relations? The goal of this process was to enable students to identify and critique neoliberal pedagogy *and* practice the creative work of constructing alternatives.

As we create ways to re-envision public spaces that we inhabit, our work is also directed toward the creation of alliances across and among classes that neoliberalism seeks to discourage. These alliances, as we have discussed through Negt and Kluge's work, must be centered around collective experiences of workers—differentiated, complex, and multiple—that form the basis for transforming social relations of capital. This approach re-articulates the identities formed around labor and seeks to intervene in the educational force of neoliberalism by disrupting its vision of market as the arbiter of equality, a vision of politics as the arbiter of law and order that "protects" this market equality, and a cultural consensus that separates the economic, the political, and the cultural that creates (even as it mystifies) labor for production.

This approach re-articulates labor and the identities formed around labor that capital encourages and that divides and differentiates social groups. As David Harvey argues, in a reading of Marx, what capital seeks to achieve is an "internalization" of the social relations of capital, "the appropriation of all manner of creative possibilities and powers of the laborer (mental and cooperative capacities, for example) that allows capital to "be" in the world at all (*The Condition of Postmodernity*, 65). It is cultural activity that, Nancy Fraser explains, recognizes and engages in dialogue with "parallel discursive arenas where members of subordinated social groups invent and circulate counter-discourses to formulate oppositional interpretations of their identities, interests, and needs" (qtd. in Warner 118).

Our particular interest is in forging alliances first by examining how everyday, personal experiences and feelings become articulated and constituted in the larger political formations of neoliberalism. Capital, as a social relation, exists at the level of personal and social relationships, in cultural spaces and practices, and in what Williams calls the structures of feelings through which we live our lives. As Williams's work in *Marxism and Literature* suggests, our analysis of the personal and the social is located in the "meanings and values as they are actively lived and felt"—feelings are social experiences, not merely personal experiences.

Coda

We realize our efforts are contingent; that is, they are linked to the material circumstances of neoliberalism in which we live and write. For example, we understand that a student-centered pedagogy that encourages students to see writing as a mode of social authority, to construct their own education, to publish and present their work in public, to re-envision the spaces we inhabit and the identities we inhabit, and to contest authoritative uses of language does not guarantee that they will create truly plural communities and publics for themselves. And, it certainly does not guarantee these efforts will not be subject to efforts of accommodation and inclusion. For example, at GW the university has become very effective at accommodating or limiting public discourse. In classrooms, public spaces, and residential halls, voices, identities, questions and dissent are silenced, ignored, explained away, or dismissed as "youthful idealism" (Riedner).

Indeed, we are often left with strategies and questions for addressing the divergent, contingent, local situations that we are faced with. However, we think these questions are crucial ones. With Mcruer, we ask ourselves and our students what it takes to move from an "anti" position where you can describe and critique what you are against to a "counter" position where you create a vision, a practice, and a politics of another world. How do we create new discourses resistant to appropriation by the logic of the marketplace, and capable of giving authority to identities, interests, and needs devalued and deformed in the market? What do terms like labor and community come to mean? How will we need to re-imagine our bodies and sexualities, as feminist theory and queer theory have suggested, if we are to become activist subjects? How will we need to reconsider our affective responses and the discourse of affect if we are to create different visions of community? How will labor need to be refigured if we are to create a truly democratic polity?

Notes

1. For discussions of neoliberalism globally, and critical pedagogy, see Peter McLaren and Ramin Farahmandpur, "The Globalization of Capitalism and the New Imperialism: Notes Towards a Revolutionary Critical Pedagogy." For a discussion of neoliberalism in an American context, see Lisa Duggan, *Twilight of Equality*. For discussion of neoliberalism and women's labor, see Grace Chang, *Disposable Domestics: Immigrant Women Workers in the Global Economy*. For a discussion of neoliberalism and disability,

see Robert Mcruer's *Crip Theory*. For a discussion of neoliberalism and the corporate university, see Chandra Mohanty's *Feminism Without Borders*, chapter 6.

2. In a Marxist theory of value that we will discuss extensively in chapter 4, value is an economic system of equivalences and social relations which capital uses and reproduces to control exchange. In the logic of capitalism, use-value is what a worker needs to sustain her life; surplus-value is that which is left over after a worker produces what she needs to sustain her life and is what capitalism exploits from workers; exchange-value is the worth that an object or idea is given in a system of exchange so it can be exchanged with an unlike object or idea.

3. Likewise, Paulo Freire argues that such accommodation is at the core of a process of dehumanization that is essential to maintaining exploitation and eliminating the possibility of radical political struggle. In his early book, *Education for Critical Consciousness*, Freire argues, "*Integration* with one's context, as distinguished from *adaptation*, is a distinctly human activity. Integration results from the capacity to adapt oneself to reality *plus* the critical capacity to make choices and transform that reality. To the extent that man [sic] loses his ability to make choices and is subjected to the choices of others, to the extend that his decisions are no longer his own because they result from external prescriptions, he is no longer integrated. He has 'adjusted' . . . [which] is symptomatic of his dehumanization" (4).

4. Likewise, Hardt and Negri argue that "the deconstructive phase of critical thought, which from Heidegger to Adorno to Derrida, provided a powerful instrument for the exit from modernity, has lost its effectiveness. It is now a closed parenthesis and leaves us faced with a new task: *constructing*, in the non-place, a new place; constructing ontologically new determinations of the human, of living" (Hardt and Negri 217–18). This "constructing" task is very much the orientation of our project.

5. For examples of how rhetorics of diversity have been used to contain dissent on college campuses, see Pegeen Reichert Powell, "Critical Discourse Analysis and Composition Studies: A Study of Presidential Discourse and Campus Discord." *CCC* 55:3 (February 2004) and Kevin Mahoney, "The Diversion of 'Diversity'" *AJAR* 1.6 (December 1998). Chandra Mohanty discusses how rhetorics of multiculturalism are activated by corporate universities as strategies of accommodation in *Feminism Without Borders*, chapter 6.

6. For a discussion of difference and value, see Gayatri Spivak, *A Critique of Postcolonial Reason*, 462.

7. Stanley Aronowitz and Henry Giroux argue in *Education Still Under Siege* that Gramsci wanted to developed an education system that "would enable children of the 'subaltern' classes to achieve not only what ruling class students learned in earlier times [hence the Latin and Greek] but also to appropriate critically the best dimensions of their own histories, experiences, and culture." (23).

Chapter 3
Circulation of Affect in University Spaces

In the previous chapter we argued that as a politics and as cultural consensus, neoliberalism is also a pedagogy: a mode of education that exists in a variety of public sites and that incorporates subjects into dominant neoliberal ideology. In universities, neoliberalism prepares students to enter into the workforce and as it does this, interpelates subjects into social relations that support the circulation and realization of capital. Neoliberalism produces structures of feeling, an imbrication of economics and social life, including emotional life.

Neoliberal rhetorics are persuasive at the level of emotion (as separate and distinct from a material base) and they are persuasive in the material ways in which they craft and direct our very "modes of life" (Marx, *German Ideology* 42). Such rhetorics shape bodies, identities, and emotions. As a rhetoric, as a pedagogy, as a theory, as an ideology, as a means of understanding collectives, selves, and their relationship to each other, neoliberalism produces bodies, emotions, and identities. Neoliberal rhetorics *do* things. As Judith Butler's work on performativity suggests, within a particular conjuncture, rhetoric produces affects by repeating norms that (re)insert subjects into a system of value, an economic system of equivalences and social relations which capital uses and reproduces to control exchange.[1] Words link ideologies to bodies, identities, and emotions and produce affects.

With Butler's notion of performativity as a background, this chapter and the subsequent one will explore the production, reproduction, realization of value, exchange, and consumption—the entire process of circulation—of emotions within a capitalist system. Emotions generate value, reproducing capital, capitalist culture, and the capitalist system of circulation. People learn to communicate in this environment in a way that is consistent with the circulation of capital in a particular context. In so doing, we are not only learning patterns of

"how to communicate in a capitalist mode," we are also reproducing the circulation and the patterns of circulation of capital itself, that is, immaterial labor.
Neoliberal rhetorics are intended to preserve, stabilize, and extend this system of
circulation, with the particular purpose of creating and maintaining workers and
consumers as appendages of capital. To create and maintain workers in such a
relationship to capital within neoliberalism, requires *material persuasion* at the
level of bodies, emotions, and identities.

Our purpose, however, is to move beyond a critique of neoliberalism,
and an analysis of the neoliberal rhetorics that generate value at the level of the
local and personal. Throughout this book, we have sought to identify points of
rupture and fissure where new political and pedagogical possibilities are created.
Our efforts are directed towards finding vocabularies and practices to respond to
the new world order: to open up value to new discursive possibilities.

This rhetorical task is simultaneously a pedagogical task: educational
praxis that exists in response to particular cultural moment, discourse, and situations. The praxis of learning strategies for intervening, reassembling, and inventing sustainable relationships of solidarity and networks that counter dominant
discourses and structures of feeling *of the particular conjucture*. As we asked in
the introduction, we are concerned with how rhetoric and pedagogy can "serve"
democratic social movements. If we are committed to deepening and expanding
vocabularies for new, critical perspectives and for democratic praxis, what pedagogical strategies can help us understand the moment that we're in? How do we
reframe our existing conceptual frameworks, walk different rhetorical pathways,
generate new modes of material persuasion, and in so doing create a "new
place" in the "non-place" of Empire?

This "new place" in the "non-place" of Empire is not a call to a certain
future, a better life, a new theory, or a forced consensus. In the introduction, we
discussed the events of A-16 as a moment in which new social practices and
lines of affinity were created. A-16 provided us with a specific opportunity to
think through the connections between pedagogical practices, rhetorical strategies, activist organization, and emergent practices of democracy. It also gave us
an opportunity, for a moment, to "undertake the imaginative task of moving out
of ourselves," a moment that revealed dominant structures of meaning and
dominant rhetorics at the same time that it engendered new rhetorical, and as
rhetorical, political possibilities, at the level of emotion and political understanding.[2]

In subsequent years, we have witnessed other potential moments of
emergent democracy—moments that seek to engender, sometimes in the space
of the university, rhetorics and practices for democracy in a neoliberal world. In
the introduction, we asked how the language and practice that the protests offered were emotional experiences that had the potential to become the basis of
lived solidarities and how could they be sustained? How do we—and we're not
just talking about ourselves here—create learning processes that disrupt the authority of neoliberal discourse? How do we create connections that Naomi Klein
suggests between militarization around the world and oppression at home? Or,

how do we create a pedagogy of the "wider context" of neoliberalism. Amitava Kumar offers us a glimpse at the kind of questions we are asking. Following Pierre Bourdieu, Kumar calls for a "different protocol of reading":

> "Who would link a riot in a suburb of Lyon to a political decision in 1970? Crimes go unpunished because people forget. All the critical forces in society need to insist on the inclusion of social costs of economic decisions in economic calculations" (Bourdieu 1998, 39) . . . This insistence is a call for a different protocol of reading. It acts with the knowledge that what one reads in a novel about alcoholism and domestic abuse among construction workers in Seoul can also be linked to the distant machinations on Wall Street and in Washington . . . Isn't the moment of pedagogy also the moment of the "wider context"? (xix)

Our point of departure extends Kumar's call for a wider context a step further, connecting the personal to that wider context. In that sense, we're calling for a pedagogy that acknowledges and seeks out the links of the personal directly to the global. We ask: who would link the emotions generated by a protest in the center of Washington, DC to (gendered) violence by the Mexican state in May 2006 to expel flower vendors from a small town in Mexico and solidarities across geographical borders that this violence engenders? This pedagogy involves connections between global decisions and policies by the State in support of capital that shape the personal as it is felt and experienced. One of the questions this pedagogy foregrounds is if global capital shapes the personal in how it is felt and experienced, the point at which it is felt and experienced becomes a site to disrupt cycles of circulation that (re) produce the subject.

Working outwards from a critique of neoliberalism, our purpose is to create and sustain protocols for reading, a part of what we have called rhetorical action, that link emergent practices of democracy, creating effective action within a specific conjunctural moment.[3] Rhetorical action, as we discussed earlier, aims at the production of new crucial literacies. Rhetorical action depends, in part, on "ingenuity, artistry and swiftness of thought," but also on a relationship to power and abilities of subject to create affective relationships in conjunction with dominant and emergent structures of feeling. Rhetorical action creates an openness for new practices and affective relationships that are already existing, but not yet articulated in a recognizable, strategic, or liberatory form. This complete re-articulation sets the stage for intervention in rhetorical spaces that are fundamental for a democracy. In this chapter, rhetorical action begins with analysis of the connections between seemingly unrelated bodily affects and emotions to global operations of capital that create and sustain value, and moving from this analysis to rearticulations that can open up networks of affiliation.

Situation, Event, Context

The following scenario from The George Washington University links the production of identity and affect, and struggles over work and working conditions to the wider contexts of power that Kumar suggests. On March 29, 2004 eleven undergraduate students at the George Washington University (GW) organized a sit-in to support adjunct faculty and service employee workers at the University, calling for living wage for minority service workers. The students were soon arrested by Washington, DC police, the result of a GW administration complaint against them for trespassing in the Marvin Center, the designated student center. This is a moment where emergent democratic practice was foreclosed. Democratic labor movement between workers and students remained emergent because it was limited by disciplining force of the university. It is also a moment to think through how this foreclosure was accomplished by neoliberal pedagogy.

Most of the students arrested were members of an organization calling itself the Progressive Student Union (PSU). Over the past few years this organization has studied, with an effort to understand, workers and working conditions on the GW campus. PSU students along with other student and non-student groups were in contact with parking lot workers in GW garages, with housekeepers who clean GW dorm rooms, with unionized cafeteria workers on the campus, and with part-time faculty who were involved in a union organizing drive. The PSU initiated sit-in was a response to labor abuses observed by the students over the course of that academic year, as well as their feeling that GW failed to respond to student objections to these labor abuses.

In the fall of the 2003–2004, it was reported that the Aramark Company, contracted by GW to operate university food services, dismissed approximately 28 of its workers. The workers—many of whom the PSU students knew personally—were replaced with non-unionized temporary workers. In addition, several food stalls in the student cafeteria were outsourced to non-union contractors. At the same time, PSU students learned from parking workers of anti-union efforts by their employer, Colonial Parking Company, the private contractor operating GW parking garages.

According to Holly Smith, a member of the PSU, PSU efforts made to develop a conversation with the GW administration about the purported labor abuses were met with silence. Students made a good faith effort to communicate their concerns to the administration by several means—writing letters, publishing editorials in student newspapers, holding rallies, and producing thousands of petition signatures. The PSU efforts to bring these labor abuses to the attention of the GW administration were largely ignored. A rally including what was termed a "dorm storming" signature drive, took place in the fall of 2003, organized on behalf of the fired cafeteria workers. The rally elicited no response from the University. After winter break, more workers were laid off. It was reported that the president of GW, Steven Joel Trachktenberg, refused to sign onto the Workers Rights Consortium, an organization established to ensure that apparel carrying the GW logo not be made in sweatshops. Campus teach-ins and performance pieces designed to raise awareness of the PSU issues failed to galvanize broad support.

On March 29, 2004, the PSU decided that an escalation of tactics was needed because of lack of response from the GW administration and the GW community. With the support of the AFL-CIO, the national union federation supporting the part-time faculty union effort, plus other campus workers' groups, the PSU held a rally in front of the main administrative building on the GW campus. After speeches by a variety of campus workers and student leaders, the group marched from the University's administrative building to the Marvin Center. There eleven students, members of the PSU, a member of the Muslim Students Association, a student from the Global AIDS campaign, two students from neighboring Georgetown University, and an unaffiliated friend, set up tents in the Marvin Center foyer. The students—who became know as the GW 11—were asked to leave by a Marvin Center manager and a GW administrator. The students declared they would not leave until University President Trachtenberg agreed to meet with them.

After they were told, "There will be no negotiations," the students once more refused a request to leave the student center. After the refusal, the Washington, DC police were called in. The students were put under arrest, handcuffed, and taken to a Washington, DC jail where they were held for over eight hours. Female students in the group where charged with illegal entry; male students were charged with illegal and disorderly conduct. Two weeks later, the student cases were heard before a Washington, DC magistrate. Without explanation, all charges brought against the students were dropped. According to students involved, the council for GW did not appear for the hearing (Holly Smith).

So how do we understand the arrests in terms of rhetorical action? That is, how do we see the linkages between the global structures of capitalism and the personal? Can we see in this moment of resistance and state/institutional violence possibilities for emergent or pre-emergent networks of affinity? In this case, how do we begin to see this as a site for the re-articulation of the "new place" and the "non-place"?

To think through the arrests with these questions as a guide, we make a detour into Gramsci. In Gramsci's work, conjunctural moments happen when systems reach breaking points, where contradictions become visible, when relationships and systems that construct the historical moment become visible, and, perhaps, when new possibilities are created in response to these contradictions. The "explicit or implicit interrelations and social effects" of the arrests tell us about the newest phase of the corporate university. It is a phase in which force along with other strategies of containment is used to silence dissenting voices and bodies (Nelson 64).

In our analysis of this moment of arrest, Gramsci's distinction between conjunctural and organic moments is particularly apt. Gramsci clearly distinguishes conjunctural moments from organic moments. An organic moment is a new phase where new structures of feeling, new political possibilities, break from the past, and, most importantly, moments when new structures would be recognized and articulated. Conjuctural moments, too, depend on organic movements, but they do not have any very far-reaching historical significance. They give rise to political criticism of a day-to-day character, which has as its subject top political leaders and personalities with direct government responsibilities.

Gramsci argues that what historical analysis must do is distinguish between organic, relatively permanent moments, and conjunctural moments, moments which appear as occasional, immediate, or almost accidental. We can gauge a shift between the conjunctural and the organic inasmuch as it shifts "the previously existing *disposition* of social forces" (our italics, Gramsci 178). So what shifts and possibilities do we see in this moment of the arrests? What dispositions are being shifted? What organic possibilities are visible? Can we begin to recognize elements of organic phenomena, "socio-historical criticism whose subject is wider social groupings—beyond public figures and beyond the top leaders"? (178). Can we see a "dialectical nexus" between the conjunctural and the organic, a movement between the immediate and the formation of a new phase?

Gramsci says quite clearly that this dialectical nexus is difficult to clearly establish and yet understanding these processes of development from "one moment to the next" for us is pedagogical work (185). At this moment, pedagogical work is involved in identifying a dialectic, the development of an organic movement and the conjunctural movement in the structure (180). How does the student action represent a dialectic between immediate, occasional and a longer, more sustained crisis of capital? In a pedagogy that links the personal to the global, we could connect this moment to other events in order to see the emergence of a new phase. What are the connections between a student fair wage campaign at an elite, Washington, DC university and the elections of leftist governments in South America, water wars in Bolivia, the "Other Campaign" by the Zapatistas in Mexico, and anti-US sentiment in Europe and elsewhere. We could see this grouping of events as a crisis of hegemony or a crisis in the coordination and maintenance of voluntary social alliances that ensure antagonistic classes internalize a set of perceived common sense interests and emotions. It is on this terrain, Gramsci argues, that the forces of opposition organize. From this standpoint, the crisis of hegemony is not something one has to wait for to emerge. The exigence is not just something that we respond to. Rather, it's already there: the work of connecting these linkages allows us to see where the crisis in hegemony is in any particular moment. Rhetorical action creates openings *through* articulating these connections.

GW is a private, urban university located in downtown Washington, DC. The University prides itself on its proximity to internships and to occupational opportunities that its DC location offers its students. GW is also one of the most expensive universities in the nation: tuition for undergraduate students is upwards of $45,000 per annum. Up to the moment of the arrests of the PSU students, GW had relied upon strategies of inclusion, including rhetorics of diversity, to interpellate students, faculty, staff, and university workers into a shared norm. There was also an effort to contain voices and identities that would diverge from this norm. GW invoked the norm through an educational rhetoric of diversity, describing the concept of university to mean a free and open space tolerant of ideas and identities historically excluded from public and university space. GW therefore prides itself in its tolerance and acceptance of different identities: there is a Multicultural Student Center, a Lesbian/Gay/Bi Student group, Hispanic Student Group, etc. However, the expectation of diversity disguises an analysis of *how* members of these groups are able to enter into the GW community. In other words, while diversity appears to offer inclusion, it diverts attention from issues of *how* traditionally excluded voices are permitted to enter into university space and how these voices are allowed to speak, even exist, within the university community.[4]

Along with the rhetoric of diversity, GW's promotional rhetoric is carefully designed to advance the idea of inclusion: political involvement, civic engagement, and critical thinking, all of which will enhance students' job prospects created through a combination of educational training, job experience, and connections generated by its Washington, DC location. According to the University mission statement, GW "dedicates itself to furthering human well-being. The University values a dynamic student-focused community stimulated by cultural and intellectual diversity and built on a foundation of integrity, creativity, and *openness to the exploration of new ideas*" (*GWU Handbook 2003–2004*, emphasis added).

At the graduation ceremony in the spring of 2004, the leader of the PSU, Allison Robbins, was awarded a prize for leadership in the GW community. In an interesting take on GW's mission statement, the university president provided a unique insight into the ways in which GW seeks to accommodate and diffuse what an "openness to the exploration of new ideas" entails. As recorded in the student newspaper *The GW Hatchet,* President Trachtenberg said, "I think she's terrific, but I think she's wrong in some cases and excessively idealistic in others and under-informed in others . . . But I think she's a great kid, and I think she is going to reflect well on the University for years to come" (Butler, Brandon).

The award was given to a student who was called "idealistic" and "under-informed" and a "kid" all in the same breath. The act of presenting the student with an award makes it seem as if the university is an open space for discussion and dialogue. Yet the award *represents* the university as a space for dialogue rather than enacting dialogue. In fact, the university president refused to meet with PSU students on several occasions. Moreover, nothing that the students had fought for had been addressed. In effect, the award co-opts the dialogue that the students sought just as the arrest forecloses their efforts to form political allegiances between students and campus workers. The award enables the university to describe itself as a free and open space, to describe itself as generous to an "idealistic" dissenter, and to claim tolerance of divergent ideas and identities. But it does this at the same time as it reminds us that students are young, not in the loop, and in a life stage where they are uninformed.

The award disguises a rigorous analysis of *why* the students were arrested and of the working conditions that they protested. In other words, the award diverts attention from issues of *how* universities exploit workers and the strategies through which they contain divergent voices from within the university community and create the appearance of consent.

Because these issues are not addressed, there is no discussion of GW's economic interests or the labor-power that underlies its educational mission. For example, GW's annexation of property in the Foggy Bottom neighborhood, rising tuition costs, and the cadre of underpaid faculty and service workers, by and large mostly African-American and immigrant communities, who provide services that make the University's educational mission possible. While this educational rhetoric invokes inclusion through the idea of the diverse community and openness to new ideas and identities, it excludes work that makes the exploration of new ideas possible. Its claims rely on the obfuscation of labor policies and constitutive relationships between labor and capital make it possible for mostly white, middle-class students and faculty to value cultural, racial, and intellectual diversity. These liberatory claims lack the complex analysis that shows how an authorized version of diversity actually preserves the status quo (Powell 452).

A secondary and largely unspoken argument is that all of these things (labor, ideology, public face of the university, etc.) are necessary to *produce* the "experience" of GW. That is, patterns of class relations and immigration and the social and emotional experience of GW are modeled as part of GW's neoliberal public pedagogy. Students are taught—not explicitly but through the institution's repeated performance of patterns of class relations and their obfuscation— to dissociate their experience with food service workers, to learn "tolerant" or "charitable" expression to African American and Latino service workers, as a means to learn how to more effectively manage a global workplace.[5] That is, this experience, and the affective relationships engendered by it generate affective value which capital corrals and reproduces. The patterns of class relationship and emotional "experience" of GW are part of neoliberal capital production: the modes of behavior, modes of relationship, the languages through which GW performs these modes, are one of the most important products of GW/neoliberalism. In several senses, by foregrounding the GW "experience"— its slogan being "something happens here"—actually describes quite well what the institution seeks to produce: a network of affective relations that performs and reproduces the kinds of affective labor demanded by neoliberalism.

We argued in the previous chapter that neoliberalism is effective *as pedagogy* insofar as it remains hidden *as a pedagogy*, as a historically specific authoritative rhetoric charged with teaching people how to be subjects of Empire. Neoliberal public pedagogy—as our example from GW demonstrates— teaches what a neoliberal identity and emotion feels like. These emotions and identities have currency within the system in which they are produced. As Sara

Ahmed argues, "emotions work as a form of capital: affect does not reside positively in the sign or commodity, but is produced as an effect of circulation . . . " (45).

Production of Consent

The use of force against the GW students is, in Raymond Williams's words, a residual moment in which a neoliberal university relies on forms of control that are now largely subsumed and transformed as part of a new hegemonic order. In other words, the neoliberal university is more interested in the discipline achieved through the leadership award than that imposed by police action. That is not to say that force is "withering away" as a form of control in neoliberalism. Rather, neoliberalism "prefers" that force, or in Gramsci's more inclusive term *coercion*, is held in reserve as a primary "persuasive" component of its rule. The use of force, in Williams's terms, recalls "earlier social formations and phases of the cultural process, in which certain meanings and values were generated" (123). In neoliberalism, instead of relying on overt and visible force to maintain control, coercion is regularized, made a normal part of policing the hegemonic borders. The current conjuncture is a dynamic moment in the expansion of the neoliberal university where force has reemerged as a regularized mode for imposing shared identities and emotions—one of the primary goals of hegemony.[6]

Gramsci's theory of hegemony accounts for the ways in which capitalist democracies have achieved consent. Force is withheld because consent has been achieved through institutions of civil society, including universities. When consent and consensus cannot be achieved by other means, there are numerous historical examples where university administrators have called in some form of state law enforcement to control what is perceived as unruly students. But of late, we are less likely to see the National Guard called in than we are to see the expansion of the university's police force, new partnerships between universities and local police, the limiting of access to university buildings, expanded powers of student judicial services, and the proliferation of cameras and other kinds of surveillance devices in university spaces and informal means of consent through grading, writing, classroom protocol, and any myriad number of regulations of spaces and bodies.[7]

This kind of normalizing seeks to make coercion *appear* as a process of consent. But as we see in the GW case, what this normalizing of coercion means is a more inflexible hegemonic border. That is, multiple identities, ethnicities, and political positions may be allowed to represent themselves—but their right to do so is contingent upon a willingness to support and buy into the basic logic of neoliberalism and its sanctioned identities. The alliance of students and workers threatens the regime of consent at GW by refusing modes of behavior consistent with the neoliberal consensus—and the state is brought in to enforce consent. In other words, this alliance threatens the production of affective values that preserve, stabilize a system of exchange. It disrupts the *material persuasion* at the level of bodies, emotions, and identities.

Consent, according to Gramsci, is possible only given the threat of State violence: Gramsci understands consent as "'historically' caused by the prestige (and consequent confidence) which the dominant group enjoys because of its position and function in the world of production," but the "apparatus of state coercive power" is held in reserve to enforce "discipline on those groups who do not 'consent' either actively or passively" (12). This violence is held in reserve until hegemony is again achieved. Williams adds to Gramsci's discussion of hegemony, noting "it is always a more or less adequate organization and interconnection of otherwise separated and even disparate meanings, values, and practices which it specifically incorporates in a significant culture and an effective social order" (*Marxism and Literature,* 115). It is the particular ways in which these "separated and even disparate meanings and values and practices" are networked through cultural institutions, through rhetorics, and through daily experiences, emotions, identities, and bodies that constitute a particular hegemony. Achieving hegemony under conditions of exploitative social relations requires "centering" the logic of that social order such that the masses consent to the terms of that social order. Reading through a Gramscian lens makes it possible to see the struggle for coherence and order as a political struggle to achieve or maintain power both structurally and materially.

For example, Gramsci makes it possible to see the intimate connection between apparent middle-class support for a market-driven culture and the unprecedented growth of the prison industrial complex. Consent and coercion operate simultaneously in support of the existing hegemony. Gramsci allows us to read the growth of the prison industrial complex, to extend the example, as a growing number of people who have either actively or passively withdrawn their consent and are therefore subject to the coercive power of the State. This is precisely what is happening in the current neoliberal context. The ruling elites, dominated by corporate owners, politicians (from both sides of the aisle), and transnational trade institutions are building—fairly successfully—"consent without consent" for a global regime dominated by the ideology and practices of neoliberalism.

To bring this discussion of consent back to the arrest of the students allows us to think about it in terms of what we learn about the current moment but also what political possibilities, what rhetorical actions, this moment suggests. The arrest of the students is a moment in which the apparatus of state coercive state power is called upon to discipline groups who will not consent. As a result, the center authority and violence of the university and the State are made visible. In this moment, the university fulfils the role in the traditions and culture of capitalism, as Chomsky says, of "regimenting the public mind" in order to ensure popular "consent" in the industrial mode of production (Chomsky, *Profit,* 53).

The active achieving of consent by institutions are acts of neoliberal public pedagogy as we argued in the first chapter. This pedagogy occurs not just in the classroom but in a complex network of social spaces where bodies, emotions, and identities are corralled by capitalism. Further, consent here relies upon the continual and repeated performance of specific affective relationships and identities. What this also means, however, is that part of "policing," dispersed coercion, is to regulate, to discipline in the Foucauldian sense, the bodies and affective relations of any neoliberal institution.

The students arrested at GW were targeted in part because of the particular identities and affective relationships they were performing in that space at the university. That is, the student union is built to reinforce the circulation of particular modes of being, identities, affective relationships: the sitting area designed to reinforce comfort and ease of conversation, the international food court as the unproblematic coexistence of cultures, and the mall-like construction of the entire student union emphasizing consumer identities where "choice" and "decisions" are mediated by the market. These students were exposing the cracks in this neoliberal space, in the hegemonic consent through their performances of "other" identities, affective relationships, and meanings of choice and decision-making.

What makes this example from GW significant, is not simply that a student action was met by police and institutional coercion. Rather, this student action is systemically connected to the neoliberal hegemony quite directly. That is their social movements, acts of organized resistance, threaten to "leap vertically, directly to the virtual center of Empire" (Hardt and Negri 58). In previous phases of capital, in the 1960s for example, the breakdown of consent was signaled by the calling in of the National Guard—the "official" expression of the State's monopoly of violence. In the current phase, coercion has been dispersed and regularized as part of the *everyday* functioning of institutions like universities. When students are met with police violence and arrest, they are meeting the face of coercion, the moment of the breakdown of hegemony, of neoliberalism directly. What we can see here is that the hegemony of neoliberalism is not complete, nor can it be, and that it needs to exercise coercion more frequently, indeed, regularly, to maintain its hegemonic status.

Hence, we link students in Washington, DC in 2004 to flower vendors in Mexico in 2006. A bringing together of GW students and the flower vendors in Mexico has to do with the normalizing of coercion as policing neoliberal consent. We're not posed to say what solidarities could emerge from this linkage, the affects that could be political groundings for networks of affinity. In fact, one of the arguments we make in this book is that these moments of normalized coercion or everyday acts that can "open a crack in history" (Marcos 216), are not simply excesses or aberrations but are the very site of rhetorical action. We don't need to wait another 501 years (see Zapatistas) for the revolution.

Notes

1. Judith Butler's notion of performativity, is "the way a signifier, rather than simply naming something that already exists, works to generate that which it apparently names. Performativity is hence about the 'power of the discourse to produce effects through reiteration" (qtd. in Ahmed 92).

2. Derrida in *Rogues*: "From Benjamin's point of view, 'democracy would be a degeneration of law, of the violence, the authority and the power of law,' and that 'there is not yet any democracy worthy of this name. Democracy remains to come: to engender or to regenerate'" (82).

3. To return to our discussion in the previous chapter, rhetorical action, as we have discussed, aims at the production of new crucial literacies. This depends in part upon the rhetor's "ingenuity, artistry and swiftness of thought," but also that rhetor's relationship to power and ability to create affective relationships in conjunction with dominant and emergent structures of feeling. The rhetor creates an openness for new practices and affective relationships that are already existing, but not yet articulated in a recognizable, strategic, or liberatory form.

4. See Pegeen Reichert Powell's discussion of diversity and access in "Critical Discourse Analysis and Composition Studies: A Study of Presidential Discourse and Campus Discord."

5. As we will discuss in the following chapter, charity sustains relations of power by empowering those who give, both aligning those who give within a hierarchical system of power, and dehistoricizing the context in which charity is given, and allowing those who give charity (but not those who receive) to accumulate emotional value within a hierarchical system.

6. As Williams in *Marxism and Literature* argues, "The true condition of hegemony is effective *self-identification* with the hegemonic forms: a specific and internalized 'socialization' which is expected to be posited but which, if that is not possible, will rest on a (resigned) recognition of the inevitable and the necessary" (118).

7. See David Coogan's "Rhetorics of Reentry" presented at the 2006 Cultural Studies and Critical Pedagogy for the 21st Century. Coogan's analysis of police action at Virginia Commonwealth University provides another example of the expansion of University Police forces.

Chapter 4
Circulation of Benevolence

*To be moved by the suffering of some others (the "deserving" poor,
the innocent child, the injured hero), is also to be elevated into a
place that remains untouched by other others (whose suffering cannot be converted into my sympathy or admiration* (Ahmed 192).

Our reading of the student arrests in the previous chapter suggests that neoliberalism produces everyday lived relationships, emotions, and feelings through
local lived experiences of neoliberal capital economy. Neoliberal hegemony,
we've argued, relies upon material persuasion of bodies, identities, and emotions. It is felt and experienced locally and personally as it achieves structural
consent. Extending this discussion here, we argue that neoliberalism is effective
insofar as it remains hidden as a pedagogy, as historically specific "structures of
feeling."

    The everyday events that characterize the lived experiences of capital-
ism, what Raymond Williams calls structures of feeling, where "our senses and
assignments of energy, our shaping perceptions of ourselves and our world" are
what constitutes "a sense of reality for most people in . . . society" (*Marxism and
Literature*, 110). As Williams's work in *Marxism and Literature* suggest, the
affiliations between the everyday "meanings and values as they are actively
lived and felt" (feelings) and systems of "world historical events" (structures)
are social *and* personal experiences simultaneously. Structures of feeling, or
what Williams calls "practical consciousness," are emotion as a way of thinking,
living, and understanding that are simultaneously produced personally, locally,
and socially.

    Particularly in late capitalism, meanings and values, the perceptions of
ourselves and our world, are produced through relations that people enter into

with one another in the labor process, the communities they establish, producing wealth and means of subsistence, and producing culture and language (Ngugi, *Decolonizing the Mind*, 13). As social phenomena, emotions are produced in the context of communication as peoples establish relationships with each other. Emotions *do* things: they locate subjects within system of power, they differentiate between subjects, align subjects with collectives (those who give vs. those who receive), produce relationships to both work and consumption, and are materially persuasive (Trimbur, John, qtd. in Edbauer, 132).

As rhetorics, we can study and pay attention to who is feeling, on behalf of whom, who is listening, and how emotions are linked to larger systems and structures. We can think through emotion to determine the most effective modes of intervention and critical exigencies for the current moment. In so doing, we can develop critical literacies of affect that articulate emotion as it is produced as a form of cultural politics. As a form of cultural politics, emotions are an opening into the social and material world: they are therefore the sites of political and cultural work and the possible site of the formation of class, the work of activism. As Williams suggests, because structures of feeling constitute a sense of reality for most people in society, they are a site to excavate the hegemonic (110) and for rhetorical action.

Ideologies of Capitalism

Postcolonial scholarship has traced the long association of cultural forms and imperial motivation. In this scholarship, benevolence has a complex emotional and social content, and a long association with the historical practice of imperialism. As postcolonial scholars suggest, benevolence is a colonial rhetoric, functioning as a discourse of conquest. Dawn Rae Davis argues that benevolence is "a gesture of saving in the name of liberation" that served in the interests of cultural imperialism (147).

Invoked in the context of imperialism benevolence is part of the material framework of colonialism as a response to perceived suffering or disadvantage of the conquered, benevolence activates social relationships that support and justify the imperial project.[1] It interpellates and translates larger political, economic, and social objectives through private, domestic, or individual relationships. In this scholarship, benevolence establishes relationships between unequally situated individuals; it configures both the subject and the object of benevolence into a relationship of power that supports the colonial enterprise.

This chapter locates benevolence in several cultural locations: a postcolonial novel, a university classroom, and the feelings (dis)associated from women's labor in diaper services. We do so to ferret out the complex affective work that benevolence does to secure capitalist hegemony. Benevolence is a historical discourse that we can see systemically. That is, benevolence has a long history in producing and reproducing colonial and imperial political, economic, and social relationships. However, benevolence is also a feeling. That is, it is a feeling felt on the personal level that immediately connects the personal with the global. It is important to distinguish between these two moments because it allows us to locate, as Kumar suggests, the global in the local and personal. We can see the global at work in the everyday. This chapter makes the connections between the discursive operations of benevolence and its operations at the level of the personal.

As an example of a discourse that activates social relationships that support and justify neoliberalism, we turn to *A Small Place* by Jamaica Kincaid. This example allows us to see benevolence's wider context in colonial and postcolonial nation-states as well as its broader status as "common sense" or "truth" in contemporary neoliberal discourse.[2]

In *A Small Place*, Kincaid describes white, wealthy members of the Mill Reef Club who "generously" donate money to poor, black Antiguans: "I believe they gave scholarships to one or two bright people each year so they could go overseas and study; I believe they gave money to children's charities" (27–28). But to Kincaid, the Mill Reef Club members are not generous. Rather, their gesture is made to make themselves feel good and expresses their selfishness: "these things must have made them seem to themselves very big and good, but to us they were pigs living in that sty" (27–28).

In this brief example, from the view point of white postcolonials, charity or philanthropy from whites to poor postcolonial black subjects is a self-less, benevolent gesture. As Kincaid suggests, no one asks why white subjects give to black subjects. No one asks what generosity signals as exchange in the context of unequal relationships of social power and in the context of capitalist exploitation. No one talks about unwaged labor as a gift and unwaged labor doesn't get counted as wealth or generosity. In the rhetoric of generosity, the social and economic inequalities of capitalism are not represented. The rhetoric of generosity, as un-self-rewarding gift-giving, does not represent subjects, labor, or violent colonial legacies.

As our discussion of Kincaid suggests, benevolence serves to define and delineate not just social difference (read: race) but economic difference (read: race and class not to mention gender) as well. It is an overdetermined discourse where the economic and cultural come together, a suturing of social relations of production that produces social life itself.[3] This suturing, we will argue through the work of Gayatri Spivak, enables us to read benevolence as (re)producing a capitalist system.

We offer this brief reading of Kincaid's *A Small Place*, not so much to examine it as "literature," but to suggest a long term rhetorical praxis by postcolonial writers to ferret out and complicate the category of "benevolence" as a discourse of capitalism. In our current conjuncture, we can see a reworking of this category of benevolence re-emerging as a dominant discourse of neoliberal hegemony. Once again, we will return to the context of George Washington University as a specific site in which this discourse of benevolence is being reworked. Further, we will examine how the performance of benevolence is not only a key point in capital's attempt to suture neoliberal social relations, but as a site of excess, a site that is open to rhetorical action.

Benevolence and Charitable Subjects of Empire

In the spring of 2003, Rachel taught a research based writing course entitled "Women in the Global Economy." The class examined gendered labor in the context of an analysis of global capitalism, investigating a variety of spaces where patriarchal, capital, and state interests converge to construct labor in terms of notions of masculinity, femininity, race, class, and (hetero) sexuality (Enloe, Mohanty, Ong, Chang). The class began with feminist texts that develop an analysis of gendered labor in the context of critiques of supranational organizations (IMF/World Bank) and global corporations (United Fruit, Levi Jeans, and Benetton). In reading of *Bananas, Beaches, and Bases* by Cynthia Enloe and *Mortgaging Women's Lives* by Pamela Sparr, students analyzed how local practices, state policies, and global capital use patriarchal and heterosexual ideologies to create gendered and racialized labor. Students became excellent *readers* of gendered labor in the context of theories of capitalist patriarchy which, as Maria Mies argues, is a system of accumulation achieved through the appropriation of the labor of women and other colonized subjects (37–38).[4]

As they became familiar with the concept of capitalist patriarchy, some students argued that a solution to gendered exploitation of women is the outside aid, charity, and generosity of First World humanitarian and feminist organizations and strategies. What women need, this argument goes, are the freedoms and benefits of a feminist first world civil society, including an awareness of patriarchal oppression and political strategies to organize against it, a state that protects the interests of its people, particularly those situated as minority, humanitarian organizations that provide emergency relief, and humane global capital which has the "ability to reform itself so that decent lives can be assured for everyone" (Ferguson, 15).

These students argued for feminism as a *benevolent* solution to gendered oppression and exploitation that is created within the complicated local and global politics of patriarchy, capital, and state. While the students read gendered division of labor in feminist scholars, their response to this concept was to offer outside aid and individual generosity of first world feminism.

In the context of university classrooms, benevolence sutures neoliberal rhetoric to affective responses of students who are being trained as mid-level workers and managers in a neoliberal global economy, putting it within the same discursive space as "tolerant" or "charitable" expression to African American and Latino service workers. This response configures a relationship of power as it establishes first world, white women as subjects who create political knowledge and third world women who receive this political knowledge. But more than a rhetoric that configures a relationship to power, benevolence is a crucial discourse and emotion for mid-level workers and managers to master as part of their neoliberal education if they are to effectively serve the reproduction and advancement of the neoliberal agenda. It is, in other words, a rhetoric—or an emotional rhetoric—which produces self-identification with hegemonic forms, an internalized socialization that appears as an individual's identity: Consent as self-identification with hegemony.

In the case of GW and other institutions of higher education, this self-identification through discourse of benevolence is part of neoliberal public pedagogy to interpellate subjects and to foreclose alternatives. The fact that there's a problem that is identified in a classroom suggests that there could be resistance. The discourse of benevolence aligns them with a much older discourse of colonialism as Kincaid suggests, while at the same time updating that discourse for the current conjuncture. In this case the work of neoliberal public pedagogy is to divert students from any possibility of challenging capitalism, to divert them from the problems posed by capital. Benevolence is being constantly and dynamically reworked to respond to new phases of capital.

This self-identification with an updated benevolence positions universities, the official pedagogical institution, to contain and accommodate social resistance. Their social function is to help consolidate the economic interests of a dominant class by creating identities, behaviors, and feelings that support these interests (323).[5] Or, as we argued in the previous chapter, their social function is to shape identities, behaviors, and emotions in a complex educational network, i.e. not just classrooms. In academic language, in official and unofficial university language, and in the classroom, benevolence gives neoliberalism authority as a feeling and self-identification.

In the context of neoliberal economic aims, benevolence functions to rhetorically delineate and consolidate a system of power and difference. As benevolence creates a hierarchy of subjects and objects, or spectators and sufferers, it marks bodies and subjects as socially different or outside the norm. Social bodies, as work in disability studies has shown, are marked as the objects of benevolent expertise. A body that is understood through benevolence/charity is a body that is "subjected, transformed, and improved" within the disciplinary institutions of the modern era. In Foucault's work, as Robert Mcruer explains, bodies are "monitored" by institutions such as universities for "signs of behavioral and physical difference that might impede their productivity; these signs of difference have been duly marked and, if possible, 'transformed and improved'" (89). Within institutions, benevolence produces docile identities within the dominant system, not bodies who will protest university labor policies and camp out in the student center.[6] When it is activated in the context of academic institutions, benevolence is not a gesture of generosity but a gesture of accommodation that, as it activates a relationship of social difference, produces consent.

Emotion Produces Value

Both the situation around the student arrests and the emergence of discourse of
benevolence poses questions of how affect works to reproduce capitalist social
relations and suture subjects to capital. The question becomes, in part, how do
we understand and think through affect not as something that is outside of or in
addition to capitalist production and reproduction but is central to its ability to
corral subjects and labor. If we say that capitalism produces nothing, it corrals
subjects and labor, then we're looking for a way to understand how this corralling happens in the everyday as subjects negotiate their relationships to capital.

In "Scattered Speculations on the Question of Value," Gayatri Spivak
argues that in Marx's work, value is an economic system of equivalences and
social relations which capital uses and reproduces to control exchange. In the
logic of capital, use-value is what a worker needs to sustain her life; surplus-
value is that which is left over after a worker produces what she needs to sustain
her life; exchange-value is the worth that an object or idea is given in a system
of exchange so it can be exchanged with an unlike object or idea.

The economic is written, it is given social meaning, a value, so that it
can operate as a system of equivalences, and, as a result, function discursively.
The functioning of value as a means of expressing equivalences in terms of social relations is where the rhetorical and the economic come together. Economic
value is decided upon in the cultural realm, entering a system of equivalences
into operations discourse, capital corrals culture.

Spivak points out that in a system of exchange, value functions as *difference*, that is, it represents something because it is not that thing.[7] Equivalency
is based on difference that is made culturally and discursively between unlike
things. However, as it creates an equivalency of unalike things in the interest of
exchange, value does not fully *represent* use-value. The concept of value cannot
stand for the labor that goes into the production of items for use-value because it
represents items *only* as exchange value. "Marx," she says, "makes the extraor-
dinary suggestion that capital consumes the use-value of labor power" ("Scattered Speculations on the Question of Value," 161). As a result, labor that is not
part of exchange is not *represented* by the rhetoric of value.

When it appropriates labor, capital appropriates use value, *representing
only* labor power. That is, capital does not see the whole person only what the
individual contributes to the production of capital. That does not mean, however,
that the person is reducible to that which is appropriated by capital. Rather, it
means that capital creates a representational system that only acknowledges the
value of the person in so much as she or he produce value as exchange-value.
This move is the representational, colonizing move of capital. It's colonizing
representation, i.e. culture. For capital, people and things matter only in their
equivalences.

This process of capital realizing value in exchange does not exhaust
human use-value. Rather, it separates out people and things that are not realized

in the process of exchange. It says, for example, we can't find a way to realize the value of child-bearing or emotional labor through exchange, so we will tie it to a different discursive economy, a different economy of value. Child-bearing and emotional labor may appear as "value," but value detached from the author-ized system of the realization of value: capitalist, commodity exchange. Capital still makes use of child-bearing or emotional labor but this labor is not repre-sented *as* labor.[8]

When production is not represented, this mis-representation of ex-change (or obfuscation of difference) has several effects, one of which is to make the foundation of capitalism in production "disappear from view" (Hall, "Culture, the Media and the 'Ideological Effect'," 323). Part of what becomes invisible from representation, from hegemonic discourse, is reproductive la-bor—which includes emotional labor—that is performed outside the market-place, most often in the domestic sphere, and most often by women. Both pro-ductive and reproductive labor and the cultural practices and feelings produced are dropped out of capitalist rhetoric.

Moreover, in this context, what is obfuscated is the value that a feeling such as benevolence produces. When subjects give, they feel good about them-selves which reproduces emotional and social value. That is, as particular sub-jects learn to "feel good" about giving, they are experiencing a capitalist class relation that directs their energies toward the authorized representational econ-omy of value and away from an "other" economy of value: an economy that builds connections among people through their interdependence and networked labor relations. That is, the possibilities of the representation of solidarity are diverted and fed back into the reproduction of capitalist class relations. The act of giving, through the discursive economy of benevolence, and the "feeling good," obfuscates labor and, thus, allows value only to be seen as that which is realized in exchange.

As we're arguing, the ideological work of benevolence is productive, it is intertwined with the circuits of capital and it reproduces the feelings that en-able this unequal exchange and relationship to take place. Within capitalism, charity without benevolence would not accomplish the hegemonic work that capital requires because it would not reproduce the dissociation between differ-ently situated subjects, it would not reproduce the obfuscation of feeling as value, and it would not foreclose upon the possibility of solidarity as a response to unequal social relations.

For our purposes here, our discussion of benevolence in capitalist patri-archy allows us to concretely demonstrate how the discourse of benevolence produces the obfuscation of subjects, identities, and labor in capitalist discourse and seeks to foreclose on alternative discourses that would contest capitalist hegemony. It also allows us to inquire into how the *feeling* of benevolence works at the level of the personal to corral the excesses produced by unequal social relations and redirect *selves*, suturing them to capitalist hegemony.

Spivak's discussion of women and representation extends the point we are making. The possibility of counter-hegmonic resistance requires an analysis that accounts for capitalism in its entirety, not simply as a system of exchange value and commodity production. In order to maintain its status as a hegemonic social system, capital must produce and corral far more than it represents in its authorized discourse. In *A Critique of Postcolonial Reason*, Spivak argues:

> the mode of production narrative is so efficient because it is constructed in terms of the most efficient and abstract coding of value, the economic. Thus, to repeat an earlier intuition, the ground level value-codings that write these women's lives elude us. These codes are measurable only in the (ebb and flow) mode of the total or expanded form, which is "defective" from a rationalist point of view. (244–45)[9]

Where representation is limited to exchange value, difference is erased. In Spivak's work, women are not represented because their work and their lives are not readable. This invisibility—as difference—is reproduced discursively. This analysis leads to an understanding of rhetoric and emotion as linked, both rooted in the concealment and dislocation of use-value and the productive process. If rhetoric—or rhetorics of emotion—leaves out use-value, then all signifying practices that give it meaning are characterized by absence. Hall points out that the rhetorics that fill out capitalism, the rhetorics that we identify with, believe in, and organize our lives around, are the site of what is hidden in capitalism: the unconscious. As he argues:

> the discourses of both everyday life and high political, economic, or legal theory arise from . . . the way real relations of production are made to appear in the form of the ideological or "imaginary" relations of market exchange. It is also crucial that "ideology" is now understood not as what as hidden and concealed, but precisely as what is most open, apparent, manifest—what "takes place on the surface and in view of all men." What is hidden, repressed, or inflected out of sight, are its real foundations. This is the source or site of its unconscious. (Hall, "Culture, the Media and the 'Ideological Effect'." 325)

All feelings, theories, images, tastes, identifications, emotions, popular knowledge, and everyday languages that fill out rhetoric are rooted in the dislocation of use-value and not represented in the discursive economy of capital. This is the unconscious of capital.

What is important to understand about the unconscious of capital is that while it may not be visible in a dominant representational system, it still circulates and has material effects. Benevolence works, materially, by corralling the excesses of capital's authorized representations into hegemonic discourse. However, in dominant discourse, benevolence appears simply as a "feeling," outside of "the most efficient and abstract coding of value, the economic" (Spivak 244–45). Benevolence does not appear to have anything to do with maintaining capitalism. But, as we have argued, benevolence *does* do work. It is this process that is not seen, the affective work of benevolence in corralling the excesses of capital, that is a part of the unconscious of capital.

For example, benevolence has a material effect: it creates a relationship between differently situated subjects, works to maintain boundaries between these subjects, and in so doing, operates as an emotion of power. It therefore shapes and defines identities for both those who "feel good" about giving and those who "gratefully" receive the gift. To extend this logic, social bodies and identities are rooted in the displacement of (emotion as) production and the material, historical and political class relationships among subjects. The affective work of benevolence seeks to accomplish this displacement.

These emotions are real—they have real effects and consequences and shape identities and bodies—at the same time as they are the site of what we don't see. When we don't recognize the production of emotion as Sara Ahmed argues we need to, emotions become "reified as forms of being," seen as natural, inevitable, or just intensely personal (12). The unconscious of capital, the productive affective work of emotion, disguises the overdetermined connections between power, material practices, and structures of feeling. As we will go on to argue, the political effect of the displacing of (emotional) value is to problematize and negate the possibility of class alliance.

Benevolence, Class, and Pedagogy

Benevolence, as this discussion suggests, sutures value to discourse in ways that allow capitalism to control and expropriate exchange and that renders labor, including affective labor, discursively invisible. To see benevolence as enabling invisibility of labor, and how it simultaneously reproduces emotional value (as a "reified form of being") we turn to a contemporary example. We will look at a conflict over an everyday, ubiquitous consumer product: diapers. We'll use this conflict over diapers as an example to expand upon Marx's idea of class and class formation in *The Eighteenth Brumaire* where he argues that class is constituted through material persuasion at the local level. In *The Eighteenth Brumaire*, Marx argues that class is formed through relations to production (work) *as well as* through material persuasion. That is, far from the more reductive readings of Marx's understanding of class, here Marx suggests that language, practices, symbolic representations, ideologies, and emotions all constitute class.

Classes are not formed naturally but are constituted historically and contextually through relationships to labor and therefore through culture. For Marx, classes are not simply a reflection of the objective position of groups of people in relation to their role in the mode of production. Rather, classes are *produced* through active discursive, symbolic, and, we would add, emotional acts. As we noted earlier in this chapter, to reduce issues of class and labor solely to their economic relations may be useful in providing a critique of how capitalism functions systematically to produce commodities, but that is a far cry from understanding how it maintains its hegemony. We turn to Grace Chang's, *Disposable Domestics*, and look at the diaper debates in terms of the labor and production that engenders emotional value that is integral to capitalism as a hegemonic system.

In *Disposable Domestics,* Grace Chang discusses the liberal debates around diaper services in California, debates that centered on the environmental consequences of plastic diapers and cloth diapers as an environmentally friendly alternative. Chang argues that these debates about the effect of diapers on the environment do not figure in the labor of women who work for diaper services and perform the reproductive labor that allow middle class women to be free of domestic work. What these debates fail to acknowledge, are the racialization of gendered labor and the class division that this labor obscures. As Chang argues:

> the conventional wisdom in middle-class mothering circles is that using a diaper service is the better option. The reasoning goes that then you can be environmentally correct . . . and it's even cheaper than disposable diapers. Few stop to ask why using a diaper service is cheaper. The answer is simple: As in most service work in the United States, the workers in diaper services are predominantly working class women of color who too are poorly paid to deal quite literally with other people's shit (and toxic detergents) all day. (35)

In this scenario of the diaper debates, women who perform labor are located as workers within a class system; women (and men) who use the diaper service are consumers. When production is not represented, when the subjects who perform labor are invisible, when emotions serve as a means of distancing subjects, the possibilities of class based on common experiences around gender are foreclosed. Gender identity, in this example, cannot be the basis of a class alliance, not to mention a social movement, because environmental concerns are disassociated from labor. In this case, the rhetoric of "environmentally friendly" forecloses the possibility of a gender-based alliance. Moreover, "environmentally friendly," carries a particular emotional relationship between the action of consuming cloth diapers and one's identity. That is, I can "feel good" about partaking in an "environmentally friendly" practice. I help, not just myself and my family, but the "world."

The discourse of "environmentally friendly" and its positive "feel good" associations gives women (and men) located within the imperial center a rhetorical identity through which to claim benevolence by using a diaper service. Middle-class consumers of diaper services claim generosity by choosing an environmentally friendly mode of consumption, while at the same moment "unconsciously" displace labor and production. Not only is class alliance foreclosed but what constitutes "the environment" is cordoned off and masked. That is, the concept of the environment is *produced* void of labor, empty of production, and as set apart from culture. This choice, however intentioned, activates hegemonic social relationships: women who work for diaper service companies and women who purchase diaper services are both inserted, differently situated, into a system of labor that is raced, gendered, aged, and classed.

In this context, emotions, more specifically the affective work of benevolence, produce a division between those who work and those who consume. Benevolence creates the consumer as "the" citizen in a neoliberal economy, in which the environment is an object of giving and generosity. Consumers "feel good" about making "informed" choices about their consumption, and "participate" in protecting the environment through their purchases. The creation of this citizen-consumer depends upon the displacement of workers and of the labor process as a whole. The emotional work ensures that no questions are asked about the workers—who make the option of an "informed choice" possible. In constructing a citizen-consumer identity focused on a construction of "the environment" as a "natural" system, these middle-class women and men address their affective energies toward that construction and away from the women who clean their shit.

The invisible and unconscious objective of benevolence in neoliberalism—whether explicitly stated or recognized—is to normalize and rationalize affects that support upward redistribution by thwarting an affective economy of solidarity that would direct the affective energies of subjects toward each other as they encounter each other in the labor process. The effect of the production of benevolence associated with middle-class consumption and the obfuscation of feelings associated with working class production is to allow capital to reproduce its economic and political objectives. Through an economy of benevolence, structural inequality, as Lauren Berlant suggests, becomes a moral opportunity for privileged individuals to express their humanity ("Introduction," 4).

This failure to recognize labor and production, and the production of emotion, is a failure of rhetoric: it is a failure of our current concepts and framing logics; an absence of vocabulary that is adequate to the task of mapping and articulating the critical possibilities of structures of feeling. This failure of language, as we have argued, is a political failure. It is a failure to recognize common social situations and relations to production, the failure of the possibility of class formation. It is not a failure of activism as such. Rather, as Diana George suggests, it is a moment where we see charity rather than activism. Our engagement and understanding does not result in "real structural change or an understanding of the systems that remain in place to keep many in poverty even while the culture at large is a prosperous one" (210). Charity is a moment that forecloses class alliance because it appears to resolve poverty without structural change. This is also a pedagogical failure to create spaces of learning in multiple cultural sites where we can develop new structures, new vocabularies, and new critical perspectives that will lead to new political understandings and create possibilities of class formation.

This absence of vocabulary, in Marx's work, emerges from a disconnection between the economic conditions that people live under and a feeling of community that could allow them to contemplate their situation in relation to others and create critical literacy. As he argues in the *Eighteenth Brumaire*:

> Insofar as millions of families live under economic conditions that sepa-
> rate their modes of life, their interests and their culture from those of other
> classes, they form a class. Insofar as . . . the identity of their interests be-
> gets no community, no national bond and no political organization among
> them, they do not form a class. They cannot represent themselves, they
> must be represented. (Marx, *Eighteenth Brumaire*, 124)

A class is *not formed*, this passage suggests, when those who share similar economic conditions do not have the literate practices to create a community of
interest. A class emerges only when "the identity of their interests" begets a
community, a national bond, or a political organization. What this suggests is
that class is as much a product of conscious human (rhetorical) activity as it is a
function of one's economic interest. Marx's argument raises questions about
why shared economic conditions do not create literate practices that would enable people to produce themselves as a class. It suggests questions for rhetorical
action and study: Are there languages that help us see affects and affective labor
as social and productive of capital? How do we create rhetorical practices that
can encourage us to develop an affective economy of solidarity? And, how can
we develop pedagogical practices—spaces of learning where we can develop
new critical vocabularies and a new praxis—that can lead to the formation of a
new class?

      This example of benevolence as a discourse and value sets up a discus-
sion of emotion as a way of thinking, living, and understanding as a political
aspect of neoliberal economy and discourse that is active in reproducing consent. As this reading suggests, emotions are cultural ideas and rhetorics which
are linked to larger political economic systems and the production of the hegemony of those systems.[10] A reading of a hegemonic discourse like benevolence
suggests, as Williams argues, that relations of domination are saturated throughout the "whole process of living" (*Marxism and Literature*, 110).

Critical Potential of Surplus Value

If benevolence is embedded in hegemony, saturated throughout the whole social
process, it is also excessive of this hegemony. As we've argued, Spivak's reading allows us to see operations of rhetoric and emotion in capitalism or, to put it
another way, to see capital as a rhetoric and emotion as a rhetoric. Spivak's
work provides us with strategies for uncovering within capital the production of
emotional rhetoric, thus opening up emotion and rhetoric into the work of difference.[11] In this sense, Spivak opens up capital to difference. This move provides rhetorical openings which, as we argue, are political possibilities.

      Because languages and emotions are part of the productive process, we
can engage emotions, as rhetorics, as modes of personal, public, or private
meaning that configure a relationship to production, that have their own internal

logic, are connected to fixed forms and ideologies, and have a dynamic history. If we think of emotions as having social and public meaning and consequences, as one of the ways in which we create thought, produce relationships, and make sense of culture, affects are a site in which to mediate and create cultural possibilities.

In a neoliberal context, as the previous section has discussed, emotions, personal responses, and identities mediate relationships and identifications between differently situated peoples. Derrida's work on *différance* can be expanded here into a materialist notion of transgression. The possibility for a creative excess exists, as Hardt and Negri emphasize, because of the excess of surplus value that capital creates. While capital contains or corrals labor, our labor is always in excess of this containment: "our innovative and creative capacities are always greater than our productive labor—productive, that is, of capital" (Hardt and Negri 146). Capital, in other words, cannot capture all of life. The creative capacity of real people always exceeds capital's ability to appropriate their creativity.

In terms of emotional labor, labor that "produces or manipulates affects such as feelings of ease, well-being, satisfaction, excitement, or passion" is always in excess of capital even while capital might seek to monopolize it (108). Yes, emotional labor is part of the current hegemony. However, emotions are also "immediately social and common," that is, excessive of surplus value (114). What we need to recognize, Hardt and Negri argue, is that this shared production can create the possibility of radical transformation and "provide conditions that make possible a project for the creation of a democracy based on free expression and life in common" (202). This suggests that for every hegemonic consolidation, or "closure," the hegemony is incomplete and creates affects, relationships, and people as in excess of the dominant hegemony.

Roderick Ferguson's work illustrates well how capital produces surplus populations and subjectivities, and by extension, how capital produces excess affective possibilities. In *Aberrations in Black*, Ferguson provides an analysis for how capital disrupts social hierarchies and these disruptions "account for the polymorphous perversions that arise out of the production of labor" (14). Capital, as Ferguson explains, produces surplus populations that exist "as future labors for capital" yet these populations "fulfill and exceed the demands of capital" (15). This surplus population was traditionally populated by racial and ethnic groups within the nation-state that were held in reserve to fulfill capitalism's need for surplus labor. However, because of capitalism's incessant need for surplus labor, it was forced to look "outside of local and national boundaries for labor . . . violat[ing] ideals of racial homogeneity held by local communities and the United States at large" (15).

In creating surplus populations, capital disrupts social hierarchies. Capital creates contexts "out of which nonheteronormative racial formations emerged" (15) through disruption, and in so doing provides the contexts for new identities, emotions and practices to emerge:

As capital disrupts social hierarchies in the production of surplus labor, it
disrupts gender ideals and sexual norms that are indices of racial difference. Disrupting those ideals often leads to new racialized gender and sexual formations. To restate, capital requires the transgression of space and
the creation of possibilities for intersection and convergence. Capital,
therefore, calls for subjects who must transgress the material and ideological boundaries of community, family, and nation. (16–17)

If we follow Ferguson's argument, capital creates transgression in excess of social arrangements, identities, practices, emotions, and bodies. This
transgressive excess cannot be contained, nor does capital necessarily wish to
contain it. We would suggest that the capital does not so much produce these
surplus populations as fail to account for its own by-products. That is, at any
moment of capitalist hegemony, capital posits the particular social formation as
the universal, final, and natural. But capital must constantly change, seeking out
new sources of labor. In order to do so, capital frequently serves to disrupt the
very categories and social relationships it once posited as universal, final, and
natural and must reconsolidate its hegemony. In this process of disruption and
reconsolidation capital is always incomplete in its ability to incorporate all possibilities of human relations. And, as a by-product of its own processes, it produces a context within which new identities and networks of affiliation arise.
What are the possibilities for agency and critique that these surplus populations,
subjects, identities, and affects offer?

The study and integration of emotion and affect into our political work
is a crucial aspect of rhetorical action. Rhetorical action on affect begins with an
understanding of the connections between neoliberalism and feeling, suggesting
possibilities for alternative spaces, alternative identities, and communication
across these boundaries. The need for specific rhetorical action, "arises most
pointedly at times when disruptions or gaps occur in the normal course of
events"—and, we would add, when rhetorical action creates such disruptions or
gaps (Hauser 6). Our analysis of emotion, value, transgressive, surplus, and excess suggests the following question: How do we develop social relationships
that are not practices of subordination? When benevolence is a dominant rhetoric through which we create identifications, how can we approach it as presenting a possibility for intervention rather than only an obstacle to class formations? What are the possibilities for transgressive transformation and class alliance that exist within, beyond, and across rhetoric of benevolence?

Beyond Benevolence

To find a language in which to challenge benevolence, we read two cultural
texts: Gayatri Spivak's preface to *Imaginary Maps* and Jamaica Kincaid's novel,
Lucy. As with our paring of classroom discussion of benevolence with Kincaid's
A Small Place, our purpose in bringing these two examples together is to locate

transgressive potential in larger political context, two seemingly different but connected rhetorical moments. In her preface, Spivak argues that she does not advocate an ethics based on benevolence because in the ethics of benevolence "responses [do not] flow from both sides" ("Introduction," xxv).[12] A benevolence that assumes that communication is possible and that subaltern women can be helped or aided is not an ethical endeavor. Rather, ethics is an understanding that communication across cultural and political boundaries is impossible. As Spivak argues:

> ethics is the experience of the impossible. This understanding only sharpens the sense of the crucial and continuing need for collective struggle. For a collective struggle supplemented by the impossibility of full ethical engagement—not in the rationalist sense of "doing the right thing," but in this more familiar sense of the impossibility of "love" in the one-on-one way for each human being—the future is always around the corner, there is no victory, but only victories that are also warnings. (xxv)

Spivak's work on benevolence provides us with an alternative language in which to think through the IMF and World Bank's rhetoric about women. Rather than seeing women as the recipients of charity or victims of poverty, we are given a language in which to consider the complex rhetorical conditions in which it is beneficial to construct women as recipients of benevolence and generosity.

In Kincaid's novel, *Lucy*, Lucy has left her family and home in the Caribbean to travel to the United States and work as an *au pair*. The novel traces Lucy's self-exile from the race/gender/class restrictions that characterize her postcolonial society to the metropolitan center. But coming to the metropolitan center as a servant, Lucy does not escape so much as live out the legacies of race/gender/class that were imposed upon the colonized world.

In the U.S., Lucy is expected to fulfill the role of gendered worker and good colonial subject. Her employer and her lover offer to educate her about the West and the goodness of Western civilization. Lucy refuses these offers of education just as she had refused to be interpellated by the postcolonial culture of her home. Separating herself from contacts in the U.S. and from her Antiguan family, Lucy struggles to find a space that is not imbricated in imperial culture. Within these hierarchical relations in the metropolitan center, Lucy must choose again whether to assimilate or exile herself from them.

Lucy chooses to identify and associate with an exile community by, as Kristin Mahlis argues, "rereading and critiquing the narratives of self-definition surrounding her" (175). She rejects the positioning of women in imperialism where women's bodies are exchanged for man's social capital. Instead, she chooses to "remove any hint of exchange or barter from her sexual encounters," rejecting gender roles in capitalism where a woman's sexuality is sacrificed in exchange for male protection (176). By refusing to participate in cultural practices of gender that valorize imperialism, Lucy forces us to rethink and see imperialism as it produces exchange value as emotion and identity. Lucy's refusal makes visible gender, race, and sexuality as affective products of an imperial system of value.

At the end of the novel, as a way to claim self-definition, Lucy has severed connections to her family and is alone in the world. Her efforts to re-write her life outside a system of exchange are not recognized as such because culturally postcolonial, black, young women are not imagined outside of race, gender and class roles. The novel ends with the following passage:

> At the top of the page I wrote my full name: Lucy Josephine Potter. At the sight of it, many thoughts rushed to me, but I could write down only this: "I wish I could love someone so much that I would die from it." And then as I looked at this sentence a great wave of shame came over me and I wept and wept so much that the tears fell on the page and caused all the words to become one great big blur. (163–64)

The blur at the end of the novel signals the closure of rhetoric as well as an opening in how we can rhetoricize this closure. The blur signals the inability of a gendered, racialized postcolonial subject to find a rhetoric that moves beyond a culturally inscribed position. The blur exists as a silence: as space that rhetoric as value cannot articulate as language. This is the "silence" beyond words that Kincaid refers to in *A Small Place* (53).

And yet the blur also suggests an interpretive opening. There is in Lucy's tears the desire for a space that is unmarked by imperialism. As Spivak observes, the blur suggests "a longing for an unmarked humanity" ("Thinking Cultural Questions in 'Pure' Literary Terms, 352). We can see in this blur the possibility of rhetorical rupture, a rhetorical revisioning that moves beyond imperial rhetoric. In this reading of Lucy, we see rhetorical action as a political and critical strategy. Reading the silences of imperial rhetoric, there is, "something there to remake" (353).

Affective Rhetorical Action

In this book, we are talking about pedagogy as rhetoric action: creating spaces for learning whose purpose is to develop understanding of new structures, giving rhetoric a place in the dynamic intersection between theory and practice with the purpose of expanding democratic, liberatory spaces of freedom. As we argued in the introduction, rhetorical action is interested in intervening in literate spaces in order to develop understandings of new structures and in so doing develop vocabularies for new critical perspectives. Rhetorical action, as we've discussed it, is a contingent, situated practice that brings theory and practice together and requires a language and orientation that reflects its particular cultural conjuncture, makes, reproduces, and remakes language and social relations.

Emotions are sites of rhetorical action and intervention. We can iden-tify relationships and common experiences that are in excess of the institution of the university or sites within the university that are in excess of its operations within neoliberalism. We can study and create critical rhetoric that pays atten-tion, as Susan Jarratt suggests, to who is feeling, who feels on behalf of whom, who is listening (or not listening) to these feelings and how these feelings are listened to. We can study how emotions are seen as personal and unpack their relationship to larger social contexts, hierarchies, emergent forms, and dominant characteristics, the work of theory. We can trace the internal logic of feelings, analyze their structure, and track their relationship to "formal or systemic be-liefs" and intuitions. In so doing, we can develop a critical rhetoric that articu-lates emotion as thought and as common. Emotions are openings into the social and material world: they are therefore the sites of political and cultural work and the possible site of the formation of class, the work of activism.

The institutional sites in which benevolence is activated are not inevi-tably hegemonic. Academic institutions, for example, are sites in which social ideas circulate and intersect with personal feelings and where "confusions and conflicts" are played out, and which are "full of contradictions and unresolved conflicts (Williams 118)." Within academic institutions, there are spaces (al-though these spaces are often subject to surveillance and rarely permanent) for dialogue, critical thinking, discussions of power and difference, and where dominant rhetorics are critiqued and re-imagined.

Notes

1. See, for example, Mariah and Paul's attempts to educate Lucy in Jamaica Kincaid's novel, *Lucy*, and in the exchange between Kincaid and the Mill Reef Club woman in *A Small Place*.

2. As Roderick Ferguson suggests, novels are a cultural form that register impe-rial power. As Ferguson argues, novels:

negotiate with the material and discursive components of African Ameri-can culture. That cultural form is the African American novel. Indeed, the material and discursive multiplicity of African American culture registers upon African American novels. As I have been suggesting, the gender and sexual heterogeneity of that culture interrogates the singularity, normativ-ity, and universality presupposed by national culture. As minority cultural forms, African American novels record that interrogation. (23–24)

3. "[T]he creation of wealth tends ever more increasingly toward what we will call biopolitical production, the production of social life itself, in which the economic, the political, and the cultural increasingly overlap and invest one another" (Hardt and Negri xiii).

4. For those who teach writing, the question becomes how to encourage the stu-dents to be writers (not just readers): to engage, participate in this discourse, not just ap-ply it but use it as a means of understanding the world.

5. For a discussion of schooling and how it trains students for the workplace, see Bill Cope and Mary Kalantizis, *Multiliteracies*, 18.

6. Bodies—queer, disabled, gendered, sexually "deviant" bodies, poor bodies, female bodies, bodies that are marked by race, age, or other social markers—are subject to subordination that produces the norm. These practices of subordination are activated by benevolence: generosity, kindness, and compassion as well as feelings of revulsion and sympathy, desire and apathy, anger and interest that all figure relationships to power.

7. Jacques Derrida's notion of *différance* resonates through this discussion of difference where representation is predicated on the absence of the referent, or the other (*Negotiations*, 189–90).

8. See Maria Dalla Costa, Maria Mies, Silvia Federici on reproductive labor.

9. Although it is beyond the scope of our discussion here, there is interesting work to be done on Freud's notion of the unconscious where an emotion is perceived but misconstrued, and where it becomes attached to another idea, and Spivak's discussion of value.

10. As Ann Cvetkovich says about trauma discourse in *An Archive of Feeling*, there is an overt connection between political economy and emotion: cultural texts and public discourse are repositories of feelings and emotions which are "encoded not only in the content of the texts themselves but in the practices that surround their production and reception" (7).

11. Jacques Derrida's, "Signature, Event, Context," provides a useful resource for our discussion here.

12. Gayatri Spivak. "Introduction" in *Imaginary Maps: Three Stories* by Mahasweta Devi, translated and introduced by Gayatri Chakravorty Spivak (New York: Routledge, 1995), xxv.

Chapter 5
Affective Intervention:
Rhetorics of Despair and Hope

The idea that hope alone will transform the world, and action under-taken in that kind of naïveté, is an excellent route to hopelessness, pessimism, and fatalism. But the attempt to do without hope, in the struggle to improve the world, as if that struggle could be reduced to calculated acts alone, or a purely scientific approach, is a frivolous illusion. To attempt to do without hope, which is based on the need for truth as an ethical quality of the struggle, is tantamount to deny-ing that struggle one of its mainstays. The essential thing, as I main-tain later on, is this: hope, as an ontological need, demands an an-choring in practice in order to become historical concreteness. That is why there is not hope in sheer hopefulness. The hoped-for is not at-tained by a dint of raw hoping. Just to hope is to hope in vain. (Freire, *Pedagogy of Hope* 9)

Our strategy should be not only to confront empire, but to lay siege to it. To deprive it of oxygen. To shame it. To mock it. With our art, our music, our literature, our stubbornness, our joy, our brilliance, our sheer relentlessness—and our ability to tell our own stories. Stories that are different from the ones we're being brainwashed to believe.

The corporate revolution will collapse if we refuse to buy what they are selling—their ideas, their version of history, their wars, their weapons, their notion of inevitability.

Remember this: We be many and they be few. They need us more than we need them.

Another world is not only possible, she is on her way. On a quiet day, I can hear her breathing. (Roy)

In 1989, Francis Fukuyama published his now infamous "The End of History?" essay in the international policy journal, *The National Interest*. In that essay, he claims that with the decline of the Soviet Union and other challenges to "liberalism," we have reached the "end of history." That is, Fukuyama argued that the "triumph of the West, of the Western idea, is evident first of all in the total exhaustion of viable systematic alternatives to Western liberalism" (3). Fukuyama's proclamation echoed Margaret Thatcher's "there is no alternative" mantra that she invoked to justify her staunchly neo-liberal reforms of the British social welfare state throughout the 1980s. In short, by the end of the 1980s there was a new, emergent dominant discursive strategy that appeared to gain the status of "truth" when the Berlin Wall fell in November of 1989 and the Soviet Union virtually collapsed in 1991.

Unlike Thatcher's crass economic reasoning, Fukuyama's argument is more interesting for our purposes. Fukuyama was not referring narrowly to the victory of liberal capitalism as an economic system. Rather, he argued that the "end of history" signifies "the end point of mankind's ideological evolution and the universalization of Western liberal democracy as the final form of human government" (4). Interestingly, Fukuyama, a noted neoconservative and apologist for neoliberal capitalism, does not conclude his essay with celebration:

> The end of history will be a very sad time. The struggle for recognition, the willingness to risk one's life for a purely abstract goal, the worldwide ideological struggle that called forth daring, courage, imagination, and idealism, will be replaced by economic calculation, the endless solving of technical problems, environmental concerns, and the satisfaction of sophisticated consumer demands. In the post-historical period, there will be neither art nor philosophy, just the perpetual caretaking of the museum of human history. I can feel in myself, and see in others around me, a powerful nostalgia for the time when history existed. Such nostalgia, in fact, will continue to fuel competition and conflict even in the post-historical world for some time to come . . . Perhaps this very prospect of centuries of boredom at the end of history will serve to get history started once again. (18)

What makes Fukuyama's closing statement interesting is that he, inadvertently we would venture, fills out an important aspect of neoliberal discourse that is often overlooked by left critiques: an affective dimension. That is, Fukuyama's "end of history" claims are accompanied by a longing—what he calls nostalgia—and despair.

This is important insofar as he provides clues to how neoliberalism claims to be the final stage of human history—*the* hegemonic social formation—and how it works to corral and contain its own excesses. Despair works to close off the ability to *think* or *feel* alternatives. Despair, reinforced by nostalgia, clues us in to how neoliberalism as a rhetoric has to acknowledge its own incompleteness. Yet, in the very same move, neoliberalism seeks to posit its naturalness and to reduce resistance or hope for alternatives, to an issue of coping. That is, neoliberalism seeks to foreclose on the possibilities of another future and creates its own "disorder"—regulating those who would think another world is possible as remnants of days gone by. Those still maintaining hope are in need of coping mechanisms that can help them become comfortable with the very real feelings of loss that the "end of history," at least as formulated by Fukuyama, generates. Is there nothing else? Acceptance, dear child, acceptance.

The status of Fukuyama's articulation of an emerging neoliberal discourse *as a discourse* is made even more apparent when we consider Fukuyama's disavowal of neoconservative allegiances and his rethinking of his "end of history" claims, most notably in his recent book, *America at the Crossroads: Democracy, Power, and the Neoconservative Legacy.*[1] However, what is important is not Fukuyama per se, but the way his articulation of an emerging, dominant structure of feeling, helped move it from the emergent into the dominant and has become part of the narrative of neoliberal hegemony.

In our discussions in the previous two chapters, we focused on how benevolence works to consolidate particular identities, displace the labor process and workers from the process of consumption, and does the affective work of suturing the excesses of capitalist hegemony. In this chapter, we will take a closer look at how despair plays a key role in the everyday reconstruction of hegemonic discourse in the face of moral outrage to social problems. We will consider how despair is mobilized as part of an emotional narrative, a hegemonic "cultural pattern of argument," that consistently leads to an *a priori* conclusion: what is, must be. We will also look at how despair does not simply work to *un-imagine* alternatives, it works to privatize democratic participation by severing communicative networks.

Recognizing Despair

Our focus on despair in this chapter did not initially arise out of our reading of Fukuyama's "End of History" essay. Rather, we began to pay attention to despair after noticing its appearance in a range of spaces in a way that closed off possibilities of imagining, or articulating alternatives to neoliberal hegemony. In particular, over the course of two years teaching an advanced composition course at Kutztown University entitled "Global Literacies," Kevin began to identify the rhetorical moves students made in responding to a range of problems posed by the course texts and in class discussions.

"Global Literacies" was a course that inquired into the language, discourse, and emerging forms of "globalization." In particular, students were to consider the new forms of literacy that were emerging and how these new literacies posed challenges to our basic assumptions about democracy, citizenship, social relationships, identities, labor, space, and time. As a course grounded in rhetorical theory, students were to explore these issues by developing a sense of the rhetorical context (i.e. what are the range of discourses, arguments, and representations of globalization) and to explore possibilities for engaging, reworking, or resisting the dominant rhetorical construction of globalization.

Naomi Klein's *No Logo* was one of the required texts for the class. The majority of the students tended to identify with Klein's narratives about her experience with brands at an early age and her accounts of working in a growing contingent, service sector labor force. Students frequently came to class prepared to discuss their own buying habits and whether or not they were "part of the problem." Many students reflected quite critically on how their own buying habits were, in effect, branded and in the process they were part of the brand. They also brought first-hand accounts of working in an era of what Klein calls, "enforced casualization" (*No Logo*, 232). In fact, the stories students told of their work experiences were often indistinguishable from the stories Klein relayed about Starbuck's "'just in time' frothing" (243), the inability to secure health insurance because employers such as Wal-Mart purposely kept their employees' hours just below "full-time" (236), or watching their parents lose their once guaranteed industrial job and end up working in the same service sector "joke jobs" that they were (262).

Klein's text provided an opening to discuss more specific issues of working conditions in sweatshops, the gendered division of labor that is accompanying globalization, the destruction of small town economies in the U.S., the depression of U.S. wages, privatization, and, ultimately, the effect globalization is having on communities in Eastern Pennsylvania. Invariably these discussions led to a peculiar yet remarkably consistent pattern of student responses. What would begin as moral outrage and identification with those critiques of sweatshops and corporate globalization, would lead to a despairing declaration: "unfortunately, that's the way it is and there is nothing we can do about it." What was completely absent from these students' responses was any hope for an alternative. For example, even those students that began to offer utopian alternatives to labor conditions in global sweatshops seemed to talk themselves out of their own alternatives almost as soon as they were uttered. It seemed as though students had the "nagging impression" that their alternatives were "always already old, outdated, and anachronistic" (Hardt and Negri 56).

The importance of this recurring pattern of student responses can be easy to miss given the all-too-common narratives of student "apathy," "conservatism," or "provincialism." In the academic environment, narratives about student "lack" or "disinterest," do more than simply reproduce a banking concept of education (i.e. we need to give them what they lack). These narratives serve as a barrier to thinking, a barrier of imagination, and, similar to benevolence, displace the actual modes of life from pedagogical inquiry. Frankly, to read student statements such as "there is nothing we can do," as carrying the same social meaning as Margaret Thatcher's "there is no alternative," or as a question of inherent cynicism or apathy reduces all similar expressions to variations on a theme, presenting barriers for rhetorical action. Such a move presents barriers, because it dissociates emotional responses from the historical, political, and discursive context within which they are made. Further, such a cynical assessment fails to consider that if these responses were simply an expression of support for the current hegemony, then there would be no need for despair. That is, despair emerges in response to a very real moral outrage that appears to have no outlet. To stay with their moral outrage, these students would have to enter the risky space of having *nothing but* moral outrage.

Paying attention to the work of despair in closing off alternative possibilities is important for political organization and resistance because too often expressions of moral outrage and despair tend to fall outside of traditional progressive/left discourse and how it has envisioned the process of political engagement. In the context of critical pedagogy narratives, Elizabeth Ellsworth has raised questions about the effectiveness of critical pedagogy's emphasis on the critical classroom being a space for "rational deliberation." In recounting a class that she taught that grew out of a series of racist incidents at the University of Wisconsin-Madison, she argues that critical pedagogy's emphasis on viewing students (and teachers) as "fully rational subjects" works against its purported liberatory goals (Ellsworth 301). In her course "Media and Anti-Racist Pedagogies," she found that following the prescriptions of critical pedagogy "produced results that were not only unhelpful, but actually exacerbated the very conditions we were trying to work against, including Eurocentrism, racism, sexism, classism, and 'banking education'" (298). The problem, she argues, is that much of critical pedagogy relies upon "repressive myths" that the "foundation of the classroom is reason" (304) often dissociated from "historical context and political position" (300).

The notion that "rational deliberation" should be the basis of political engagement has a long history in progressive thinking. In George Lakoff's recent book, *Don't Think of an Elephant*, he takes issue with several liberal and progressive "myths" that are detrimental to a progressive political agenda. One of these key myths grows out of a commitment to Enlightenment's reliance upon rational deliberation. Lakoff lays out the narrative of this myth as follows: "The truth will set us free. If we just tell people the facts, since people are basically rational beings, they'll all reach the right conclusions" (Lakoff 17). Drawing from his work in cognitive linguistics, Lakoff argues that this approach begins from the faulty premise that facts somehow speak for themselves. However, concepts and by extension, modes of thinking about the world, are "not things that can be changed just by someone telling us a fact" (17). For new concepts, alternative possibilities to be even intelligible, they must fit our conceptual frames. If they don't, the "truth" will simply "bounce off" and not be integrated into our ways of understanding the world.

The fact that progressives find themselves continually frustrated with what appears to be the majority of people's "irrationality" in the face of "the facts," says more about how progressives understand political action than it does about people's degree of rationality. For example, a myth that grows out of this Enlightenment commitment to rationality is that a "normal person" will make decisions based upon her or his self-interest. Yet, when working class voters turn out in support of conservative Republican candidates—candidates who will no doubt support further privatization and cutting of the resources most working class Americans rely upon—progressives are "shocked or puzzled" (18). Lakoff argues instead that progressive confusion is a result of their faulty assumptions about politics, not because most working class Americans are dysfunctional. Rather, he continues, "people do not necessarily vote in their self-interest. They vote their identity. They vote their values. They vote for the person with which they can identify" (19).

Lakoff's stated agenda in this book is to assist progressives in articulating progressive values, a "clear moral vision," so that Democratic candidates can win elections in the future (xvi). Lakoff is interested in "reframing" particular messages so that they "activate" an already existing progressive frame. In particular, much of his recent work has been devoted to exploring two competing frames based upon "the family." The family is important, according to Lakoff, insofar as much of our language about nation is framed in terms of a family unit. A problem with Lakoff's analysis from our standpoint is that the metaphor of "nation-as-family" reinscribes the nation at the primary site of political engagement—a site that is becoming increasingly problematic in the face of neoliberal globalization and that does not help to explain the kinds of shifts in sovereignty, labor, and capitalist hegemony that we are interested in. However, his project is important in that he argues that "[r]eframing is changing the way the public sees the world. It is changing what counts as common sense. Because language activates frames, new language is required for new frames. Thinking differently requires speaking [or writing] differently" (xv, brackets ours).

What's important for our discussion is that when it comes to engaging in situated rhetorical action—be it in the classroom, campaigning for an electoral candidate, or organizing against the World Trade Organization—there are limits to privileging rational deliberation and marginalizing the crucial work of affect in maintaining hegemony. What we risk is accepting a reductive narrative of Enlightenment rationality and engaging in a missionary politics seeking to "bring the light" to those who are "in the dark." Very often progressives and left activists, scholars, and teachers unconsciously assume a notion of false consciousness that requires only the light of rationality, the facts, or the truth to emerge from the cave. As Ellen Cushman argues, when the language and practices of everyday people are "judged through the lens of false consciousness, hegemony seems to be sustained by acquiescing dupes who themselves are responsible for their own domination" (8). The notion of false consciousness that Cushman critiques, has certainly been widely problematized, but the lack of attention to the work that lived emotions do in maintaining hegemony, suggests that some of its assumptions still inform progressive politics.

As we have suggested, Raymond Williams argues that a "fact about modes of domination" is that "no dominant social order and therefore no dominant culture ever in reality includes or exhausts all human practice, human energy, and human intention" (*Marxism and Literature,* 125). We would extend his argument by suggesting that the excess of human practice, human energy, and human intention does not reside in the hands of a small group of people in a Platonic-esque Republic, leading the masses out of the darkness. Rather, this excess is dispersed and reworked in the everyday through our interaction with that hegemony. Williams argues further that this excess, what is excluded from the dominant hegemony, "may often be seen as the personal or the private, or as the natural or even the metaphysical" (125). That is, what can often be seen as "emotional" discourse that does not "hold up" under rational scrutiny, may be a site in which the excesses of neoliberal hegemony are finding voice. The fact that in "advanced capitalism," as Williams argues, "the dominant culture reaches much further than ever before . . . into hitherto 'reserved' or 'resigned' areas of experience and practice and meaning" (125–26) suggests that for neoliberal hegemony to be maintained, it must ratchet up its attempt to corral the excesses that it produces.

As we have suggested thus far, the work of despair helps resolve an excess of neoliberalism, namely that gap produced between its conditions of production and the moral response of individuals confronting those practices. But despair is also important to engage if we recognize, as in the case of benevolence, the process of dislocation that despair accomplishes is more than a way of unimagining alternatives. Rather, excesses of emotion are inscribed into a dominant hegemony "when they are lived, actively, in real relationships" (130). That is, despair works not only at the level of an individual's consciousness, but structures that individual's relationships. Despair becomes a *shared cultural discourse* that contradictorily isolates individuals from each other as it corrals them into a shared response to neoliberal hegemony.

Neoliberal Despair:
Mapping the Reproduction of Hegemony in the Everyday

If, as we have argued, despair helps contain and corral an excess of neoliberalism, it is important to take a closer look as to how despair works as part of a larger cultural discourse. That is, as we have argued, despair is an affective response to "moral outrage" to abusive and exploitative conditions that run counter to an "other" common sense. Despair plays a crucial role in arresting a subject's desire for an alternative, and transforming an opportunity for imagining into a seemingly novel "realization" that such a desire is fool-hearty. What we see in the everyday working of despair, is the work of hegemony at the level of *habitus*—"a system of lasting, transposable dispositions which, integrating past experiences, functions at every moment as a *matrix of perceptions, appreciations, and actions*" (Bourdieu, *Outline*, 82–83). That is, despair is not limited to one specific kind of experience within neoliberalism. Rather, it is a transposable disposition, flexible enough to contain expressions of resistance. As part of a hegemonic discourse, despair sneaks into everyday arguments about current conditions and possible alternatives.

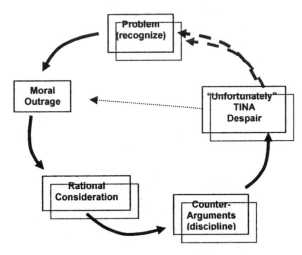

Figure 1

The fact that we have noticed despair articulated and felt in a range of sites, suggests that it is a kind of cultural pattern of argument, a script laying out how to *be*, how to *cope* within a neoliberal world. Returning to the kind of responses students made in Kevin's class will allow us to get a sense of what this script looks like. Take the issue of sweatshop labor, for example. The despair script begins with the awareness of a problem, or the recognition of a particular condition *as a problem* (See figure 1). Case studies and descriptions of sweatshop labor, rarely present themselves as unproblematic: women being forced to abort babies, mandatory twenty-four-hour days, lack of bathroom privileges, child labor, etc. The problem appears *as a problem* because it does not conform to what is considered good, just, moral, or right for a particular individual or group. In short, sweatshops do not conform to a set of values.

Initially, as we suggested earlier in this chapter, the expression of that disjuncture between a subject's values clashing with the "values" of sweatshop labor and the connections between that labor and that subject's implication in global divisions of labor through their consumption, produces a range of emotional responses including guilt, shame, and, in our example here, moral outrage. We want to focus on moral outrage here because it is clearly an example of an exigence—a moment that calls for a response, and is open to explanation and resolution. In short, it marks a moment that is open to rhetorical re-scripting. But, as we will suggest, resolving or providing a frame of reference for engaging the problem affirmatively, quickly becomes problematic.

Moral outrage does not necessarily provide a conceptual framework in which to place the problem. At the same time, we do not believe moral outrage to be disingenuous. That is, an expression of moral outrage is *real*. While there are certainly cases of moral outrage that are merely socially acceptable responses, politically correct responses, we are much more interested in those occasions in which moral outrage is a genuine response to becoming aware of a problem such as sweatshops. Moral outrage is expressed through responses such as "that's just wrong," "I can't believe anyone could do that to another person," "I can't take part in this," or "something has to be done to stop this!" Such responses invoke both a broader set of values and a negotiation of identity. On the one hand, the judgment "that's just wrong" draws upon "a system of lasting, transposable dispositions" that is brought to bear upon "an *objective event* which exerts its action of conditional stimulation calling for or demanding a determinate response" (Bordieu, *Outline*, 83). On the other hand, the demand for a response is only "heard" by "those who are disposed to constitute it as such because they are endowed with a determinate type of dispositions" (83).

Such moments are what we might call *micro-negotiations* of hegemony insofar as they are small moments of negotiation in which an individual has to adjust, or not adjust, her or his relationship to the dominant social form. As Williams suggests, hegemony is

a whole body of practices and expectations, over the whole of living: our senses and assignments of energy, our shaping perceptions of ourselves and our world . . . [It is] a lived system of meanings and values— constitutive and constituting—which as they are experienced as practices appear as reciprocally confirming. (*Marxism and Literature*, 110)

These micro-negotiations of hegemony are important in that they are a site of active negotiation, updating, and reconstitution. In particular, we can recognize that part of what is happening in moments of moral outrage, is the (re)constitution of particular forms of identity. This is not to say that hegemony is simply the accumulated micro-negotiations of individuals. Rather, when we can see patterns in how people respond to challenges to neoliberal hegemony, we can better understand the rhetorical strategies of neoliberalism.

As figure 1 demonstrates, what happens next is a move from emotion and to rationality. It is at this point that subjects begin to "test" their moral outrage against "the facts," but more importantly, the facts as they are framed within neoliberal discourse. Two things happen here. First, the dominance of neoliberal arguments, the sheer number of instances they are encountered on a daily basis, frame neoliberalism and our example of sweatshops as the "real." However, many of these arguments can seem suspect in the face of the moral outrage an individual is feeling. That is, despite the rational and pervasive arguments defending sweatshops, or, more likely, defending the neoliberal division of labor that requires sweatshops, someone who is appalled by the conditions in those sweatshops, is not necessarily receptive to neoliberal apologetics.

What is significant in the second aspect of this shift from outrage to rationality has to do with the institutional dominance of "rational deliberation" that Ellsworth problematizes. She argues that in schools, "rational deliberation, reflection, and consideration of all viewpoints has become a vehicle for regulating conflict and the power to speak, for transforming 'conflict into rational argument by means of universal capacities for language and reason'" (Ellsworth 301).[2] While Ellsworth is referring specifically to schooling, weighing arguments, listening to all sides and then making up one's mind has a long history in Western culture and is made use of quite effectively in the reproduction of neoliberal hegemony. The dominance of rational deliberation works to dissociate the response of outrage into the more disciplined space of rational discourse. As Williams suggests, the excesses of hegemony "may often be seen as the personal or the private" (*Marxism and Literature*, 125). The shift into rational discourse here marginalizes outrage as something that is a "personal" response that is not appropriate for "public," rational deliberation.

Once there has been a shift from emotional to rational debate, the groundwork for despair has been laid. In Kevin's class, he found that once students were asked to consider alternatives within a framework of rational deliberation—a framework that in many cases he was responsible for introducing—students quickly started to make despairing statements such as "there is nothing we can do," or, in the case of sweatshops, "maybe people in other cultures do not find it so bad . . . maybe those conditions are actually better than the ones they had before." To try and better understand what happened once rational deliberation was introduced, the class spent a significant amount of time discussing their despair. The model represented in figure 1 is a product of those discussions. What appears at first as a retreat to "there is nothing we can do" in order to avoid thinking about possible alternatives, is actually a rather complex process of considering all of the counter-arguments to their outrage. Briefly, students were already armed with a battery of responses that dismissed or rejected any resistance to neoliberal hegemony. In particular, students seemed to chastise *themselves* as being "idealistic," "not considering all options," or as "overreacting" to what they first read. "Rational" arguments in favor of sweatshops provided a discourse that both disciplined their responses and armed them with a discourse of power—that is, a discourse that was valued within neoliberal hegemony.

However, these hegemonic arguments and identities still leave an affective excess. Providing individuals with a discourse that sutures them to neoliberal hegemony is one thing. However, transforming a system of values so that one can argue sweatshops are *moral, right, just,* and *good,* is another matter entirely. Once neoliberal hegemony has been affirmed through rational deliberation, it leaves a gap between these rational conclusions and the affective response of outrage that has much deeper roots in social identities and systems of values. Thus, when there is a gap between these rational conclusions and the *feelings* of what is moral, right, just, and good, it is not just a contradiction between the head and the heart, but a contradiction in a subject's understanding of her or himself as moral, right, just, and good.

Despair provides a way of reconstituting a subject's identity by allowing for a rational acceptance of sweatshops, for example, while reclaiming that subject *as* moral, right, just, and good. The subject can *know* what's moral and just, but is *unable* to activate his or her sense of morality and justice because he or she has no choice. Subjects are, in a sense, victims too. In order for subjects to reconstitute themselves as moral subjects, they need to concentrate only on their most immediate actions, what they can control which is, after all, themselves. The moment of despair, deflects the imagining of alternatives to sweatshops back onto the self and her or his desires. Another rhetorical path open, but one that still maintains hegemony, is to return to moral outrage as a matter of will. In that move, while individuals may resist despair, they reaffirm their status as an irrational Other that refuses to accept reality and that is in need of, as we suggested at the beginning of this chapter, better ways of coping.

What is remarkable in this pattern of outrage and despair, is how closely it mirrors Fukuyama's "End of History?" essay with which we began this chapter. Fukuyama closes his essay with a personal narrative about his own despair, and offers what can only be seen as a moment of wishful thinking that "centuries of boredom at the end of history will serve to get history started once again" (18). Despair, and nostalgic self-reflection, closes off opportunities to imagine alternatives and to ask questions about what might constitute joy or hope at this conjuncture. Instead, neoliberal hegemony is able to reaffirm its status as what is and what shall be in the silence of despairing subjects. Before we move to discuss how this very moment of despair can be an important site of rhetorical action, we first want to engage how this cultural argument of despair seeks to privatize democratic participation by severing communicative networks.

Internalizing the Public: Democratizing Domination

The kind of close analysis of discursive moves individuals make in negotiating neoliberal hegemony we have just discussed, is, of course, not how these negotiations take place in the everyday. If the discursive pattern of outrage and despair were more explicit *as a pattern*, then it might be easier to engage and critique. However, the complexity of these discursive moves is, more often than not, negotiated *internally* outside of public spaces. Kevin's work with students was able to "map" some of these discursive moves through students' repeated performance of this particular discursive negotiation. What became clear was that much of the "rational deliberation" takes place internally, unarticulated in a broader communicative network. That is, the weighing of arguments, allowing for other voices to engage, critique, add, and support a particular position, is performed in a kind of internal public sphere—but a public sphere that is not "public" in the strict sense.

In his book *Emergent Publics*, Ian Angus argues that strong democracy requires "access to public *places* where give-and-take of discussion allows each citizen to form his or her opinion" (25). The rise of mass consumer culture and the privatizing of public space, has contributed not only to a decline in public places, but a "loss of civic discourse"—a "process of sharing, criticizing, and modifying . . . opinions in a continuous given-and-take" (34). While we would agree with Angus's general argument, we believe that the problem posed by neoliberal hegemony for democracy is not simply a matter of a loss of public places and civic discourse. Rather, the problem is also one of *how* democracy itself is reworked and privatized. More specifically, how the notion of a public sphere as a space of *rational discourse*, of argument and counter argument,[3] is cut off from actual spaces and is internalized in a performance of democratic deliberation.

In *Empire* Hardt and Negri argue that the present order is characterized by a passage to the "society of control," in which the "mechanisms of command become ever more 'democratic,' ever more immanent to the social field, distributed throughout the brains and bodies of the citizens," and the "behaviors of social integration and exclusion proper to rule are . . . increasingly interiorized within the subjects themselves" (23). The model represented in figure 1 is, in this sense, a map of the *internalization of democratic deliberation* with the resolution of the deliberations already accounted for by neoliberal hegemony. The process of democracy, as opposed to the formal institutions of democracy, requires communicative networks that promote public deliberation. However, transforming outrage into despair by internalizing the process of *rational* democratic deliberation, cuts off these communicative networks. Instead of individuals engaging in a discursive exchange, they are transformed into individuals deliberating privately with the detached discourses of neoliberalism *along side* each other. That is, the communicative networks that would promote solidarity, creativity, and connection, are substituted by deliberation with the disembodied discourses of neoliberalism masked as private, self-questioning. Despair not only short circuits the possibilities of imagining alternatives, it is also a way of relating to other subjects—other subjects, who like Fukuyama—mirror a similar sense of despair.

Ironically, in this collective experience of despair lies great potential for rhetorical action that is undetectable from traditional progressive approaches to political organization. Despair in isolation produces another desire—a desire to belong, to connect, and to be happy. In this context, it should not surprise us that more and more Americans—especially younger Americans—have turned to religion in their search for community. Religion speaks to the self, to the "soul." The desire for community and for happiness may be momentarily, and repeatedly, deferred by despair, but it is not contained. Relations of solidarity produced by social movements offer a space to respond to that desire. As Angus argues, "it is through social movements that the isolated and competitive individual can be surpassed by an individual sustained and recognized within an active community" (41).

The question then becomes what kind of social movements? As we have argued throughout this chapter, many of the traditional progressive and left movements have relied upon the very practices that contribute to a politics of despair. It would be naïve to simply posit social movements as a panacea for neoliberal despair. If neoliberalism is reproduced, in part, through individuals' micro-negotiations with its hegemonic discourses, then those micro-negotiations may also be fruitful sites for political engagement. That is, the presence of despair is also an exigence for rhetorical action. In the remaining pages of this chapter, we will discuss some possibilities for how to engage in *affective* rhetorical action. In particular, we will be looking at the role of cultural production as a mode of counterhegemonic rhetorical action.

Affect, Narrative, and Networks of Social Relations

In his essay, "Putting Emotions in Their Place," Craig Calhoun argues that emotions have been marginalized in the study and, we would add, rhetorical strategies, of social movements. This happened, he suggests, "to a very large extent, in reaction against a tradition of collective behavior analysis . . . [which] approached collective behavior mainly from the outside, as something that irrational others engaged in" (Calhoun 48, brackets ours). However, in seeking to affirm collective action as "rational," long traditions of political analysis and praxis were thrown out (48). Calhoun recalls that both modern utilitarian thinking and the Scottish moralists, including Adam Smith, were "concerned with historical, cultural, and social structural variations in the ways in which emotional bonds and lines of conflict were institutionalized" (50). Out of these traditions also grew Gramsci's notion of common sense. For these political theorists, common sense was, as Gramsci also argued, "a capacity to achieve common understanding shaped by feeling as well as thinking" (50).

The move to assign emotions, social relations of connection, love, and solidarity, to the sphere of "the irrational" in Western thought is as old as Plato's metaphor of the passions as unruly horses that need to be controlled and tamed by a charioteer in *Phaedrus* (149). Recent reconsiderations and rereading of the Sophists have called attention to the ways in which Plato's construction of the binary between rationality and emotion, mind and body, and philosophy and rhetoric laid much of the foundation for Western rationality, especially with the reclaiming of Plato at the onset of modernization. As Susan Jarratt argues, "Plato's exclusion of rhetoric in favor of philosophy stands as a prototype for the process of displacement that characterizes Western philosophy" (*Rereading*, xxiii). As we argued in the last chapter, this displacement is not simply a philosophical matter. The displacement of emotion to the sphere of the irrational, is also the displacement of emotion as cultural production and the material, historical, and political class relationships among subjects. This displacement is the work of neoliberal hegemony.

One of the questions raised by the discursive work of despair in maintaining neoliberal hegemony is how to intervene in that pattern of discourse to disrupt its seamless reproduction and to open a space for imagining alternatives. We have suggested that there are limits to the role of rational debate, allowing the "truth" to set us free, and rhetorical strategies that do not engage despair and

emotions more broadly as real, material, and intertwined with the important affective work of social movements in creating economies of belonging, solidarity, and community.

Such a question is even more important when we consider Calhoun's
suggestion that "institutions, and organizations, and relationships all gain their
relative stability in part from people's emotional investments in them. In other
words, we have huge emotional investments in the everyday status quo" (54). In
recognizing such investments, we also need to work carefully with what it
means to disrupt or challenge the everyday patterns of discourse that maintain
neoliberal hegemony. That is, we suspect, that these emotional investments in
the status quo better account for why individuals do not immediately reject despair and look for hope. Hope, when not connected to a counterhegemonic network of relations, is a risky place to be. As Paulo Freire argues, hope is a necessary part of political struggle:

> the attempt to do without hope, in the struggle to improve the world, as if that strug-
> gle could be reduced to calculated acts alone, or a purely scientific approach, is a
> frivolous illusion. To attempt to do without hope, which is based on the need for
> truth as an ethical quality of the struggle, is tantamount to denying that struggle one
> of its mainstays. (*Pedagogy of Hope*, 9)

However, "the idea that hope alone will transform the world, and action under-
taken in that kind of naïveté, is an excellent route to hopelessness, pessimism,
and fatalism" (9). Hope without an "anchoring in practice in order to become
historical concreteness" (9) can actually contribute to a deepening of despair
since it is hope without a context.

Freire's notion of critical hope, hope that is anchored in practice, suggests that to intervene in neoliberalism's production of despair, we cannot simply posit hope as a counter to despair. Further, in order to intervene in the discursive frame that supports despair and to resituate the micro-negotiations of
hegemony toward relations of solidarity and hope, it's important to begin to engage in a process of building critical hope through counterhegemonic discursive
frames. In "Finding Emotion in Social Movement Processes," Anne Kane discusses the process through which a collection of diverse social groups in Ireland
in the late 1800s built a social movement known as the "Irish Land Movement."
This social movement led to the "immediate restructuring of the Irish land tenure system and soon afterward to the dismantling of landlordism in Ireland"
(Kane 251). Kane's work pays attention to the ways in which the Irish Land
Movement was able to create political solidarity and alliances through "the construction of symbolic systems of meaning" (251). In particular, Kane argues that
these alliances were made possible through the "narrative reconstruction of
meaning" (252). Paying attention to the narrative is important because the
"structure of narratives is often based on metaphoric conceptualizations of emotions" and through a gradual process of transforming these narratives, it was

possible for diverse groups to imagine themselves in alliance while preserving and/or transforming their emotional investments (252).

What Kane's analysis suggests is that rather than engaging in a process of "rational deliberation" that seeks to (rationally) convince diverse groups of people to resist the landlord system through an appeal to their "objective" interests, the counterhegemonic narrative work of this movement addressed the rational and the emotional as inseparable. Over time the Irish Land Movement was able to transform "the 'master narratives' of emotions which prevailed among the Irish at the beginning of the Land War—narratives of humiliation, shame and anger" which led "to reconstructed emotions and militant movement action" (255). This transformation took place through "monster meetings,"—"massive land meetings which took place every week, sometimes up to ten meetings on any given weekend" (256). Like an early industrial polis, these land meetings were a site for public negotiation of the meaning of the land tenure system, but with the object of "symbolic and meaning construction" through re-narrating the meanings of deeply held emotional investments (256). Kane demonstrates through an analysis of documented speeches, primarily in the form of "narratives, recounting essential Irish history and myths," (256) how the Irish Land Movement transformed the narratives of Irish humiliation into narratives of collective power. These public re-tellings of Irish history, were infused with emotional work:

> The most prevalent emotions [in the speeches] are shame, fear, sorrow, humiliation, indignation, disgust, anger, hatred (of England and landlords), love (of Ireland and the land), pride, empowerment, enthusiasm, solidarity, vengefulness, and righteousness. Clearly the emotions in the first half of this list are almost the opposite of those in the latter part. The former emotions, specially shame, fear, sorrow, and disgust, formed a 'habitus of humiliation' shared by the Irish as the land movement began; the growing hatred, anger, and indignation are emotions demonstrated in hundreds of narratives as the land movement grew; and these emotions, nurtured by narrative sharing and movement activity, blossomed into emotions of solidarity, enthusiasm, pride, love, and empowerment, greatly solidifying the alliance of movement participants and contributing to the success of the movement. (256–57, brackets ours)

While it would be too much of a distraction to go into all of the particulars of Kane's analysis here, we want to draw attention to parts of her analysis that can help shape rhetorical actions as we engage hegemony.

First, the Irish Land Movement addressed the "habitus of humiliation," through telling stories drawing from a collective experience of that humiliation. Drawing from shared cultural narratives about Ireland and being Irish, the stories told at "monster meetings" provided an outlet for the shame, a public space to experience the shame openly and collectively. Thus, the narrative of shame was allowed passage from the internalized space of the self, to a public space of collectivity. In that process, the narrative of shame itself could be reworked.

And Kane suggests that such a public participation in reconstructing this emotional master narrative did occur:

> As local and national newspapers gave almost verbatim accounts of both "monster" and branch meetings as well as eviction processes, demonstrations, and court proceedings, virtually everyone in the country became involved in the discursive contention and meaning construction of the land movement. (256)

In a sense, we can see the Irish Land Movement as an instance of a re-understood public sphere that did not accept a separation between the rational and the emotional. Rather, an emotional rationality and its narration were key aspects of this "public."

Secondly, and crucially, the narrative reworking, the "discursive contention and meaning construction," was "anchor[ed] in practice . . . [and] historical[ly] concrete" (Freire, *Pedagogy of Hope,* 9). Once the narrative of shame was made public, people were not left alone in their vulnerability. Shame, in the Irish context, however destructive and alienating, was part of an "emotional habitus," which, as Calhoun argues, is part of the "characteristic ways of relating emotions to each other, and of relating emotions to cognition and perception" (53). That is, to disrupt the narrative of shame calls into question those very modes of relating. Social movements such as the Irish Land Movement upset the seamless reproduction of routine modes of relating. Such "nonroutine action," Calhoun argues, "removes some of the everyday social relationships in which emotions are invested stably and gives occasion for the workings of other emotions or other patterns in the appearance of emotions" (55).

Kane's analysis suggests that reworking emotional master narratives alone does not provide for patterns of solidarity, love, and belonging. Rather, it is the reworking of these narratives collaboratively and connected to organizations, processes, and communities in the process of political struggle that anchors emerging, counterhegemonic narratives in practice. The collective reworking of emotional master narratives in this way is a form of collective cultural production that stands in direct opposition to the reproduction of the existing social order.

Reworking emotional master narratives is perhaps even more important in the space of neoliberal hegemony and its discourses of despair insofar as "mechanisms of command become ever more 'democratic,' ever more immanent to the social field, distributed throughout the brains and bodies of the citizens," and the "behaviors of social integration and exclusion proper to rule are . . . increasingly interiorized within the subjects themselves" (Hardt and Negri 23). That is, as the hegemonic becomes more and more focused on managing and corralling affective relations and labor, it becomes even more important to resist the splitting off of emotion from rhetorical action. In the case of despair, Kane's attention to the reworking of emotional narratives, points in the direction of how we might begin to engage the micro negotiations of the hegemonic in the everyday.

As a form of rhetorical action, reworking of emotional master narratives also suggests that it is important to consider how we understand to whom we are speaking. As we argued above, despair produces both a disruption of communicative networks that are essential for solidarity and a desire for connection. This suggests that focusing too intently on disrupting the explicit "public" arguments of neoliberal hegemony, may be misplaced, or at least, only part of the picture. In their critique and reworking of Habermas's notion of the bourgeois public sphere, Oskar Negt and Alexander Kluge argue:

> as soon as the worker participates in the bourgeois public sphere, once he [sic] has won elections, taken up union initiatives, he is confronted by a dilemma. He can make only "private" use of a public sphere that has disintegrated into a mere intermediary sphere. The public sphere operates according to this rule of private use, not according to the rules whereby the experiences and class interests of workers are organized. The interests of workers appear in the bourgeois public sphere as nothing more than a gigantic, cumulative "private interest," not as a collective mode of production for qualitatively new forms of public sphere and public consciousness. To the extent that the interests of the working class are no longer formulated and represented as genuine and autonomous vis-à-vis the bourgeois public sphere, betrayal by individual representatives of the labor movement ceases to be an individual problem . . . In wanting to use the mechanisms of the bourgeois public sphere for their cause, such representatives become, objectively, traitors to the cause they are representing. (Negt and Kluge 7, brackets ours)

If the dominant public forces a fracturing of collective articulations into sets of "private" interests, this presupposes some kind of process by which individuals have articulated themselves within a collectivity, what we might call a rhetorics of solidarity.

The process of producing counterhegemomic narratives, as Kane suggests, is a mode of producing and sustaining collectively insofar is it asks for participation and addresses the "whole person" as well as the affective labor that makes solidarity possible. In contrast to participating in the dominant public sphere, Negt and Kluge propose challenging hegemony through "the counter-products of a proletarian public sphere: idea against idea, product against product, production sector against production sector" (79–80). What becomes foregrounded is not the dominant hegemony, but rather the creative possibilities of people in their modes of life. That is, rhetorical action, specifically reworking emotional master narratives, *is* counterhegemonic cultural production. But in order for such work to be recognized as such, it becomes important to map the affective work of neoliberal hegemony as we have been doing in these last three chapters.

In the last chapter, we turn our attention to two traditions of rhetorical action and how these traditions offer promise for counterhegemonic struggle for the next century.

Notes

1. An excerpt from *America at the Crossroads*, was reprinted as the essay, "After Neoconservatism," in the Feb. 19, 2006 *New York Times*. In that essay, Fukuyama offers a pointed attack on both the neoconservative legacy and the Bush administration's war in Iraq.

2. In this passage, Ellsworth is quoting Valerie Walkerdine's "On the Regulation of Speaking and Silence: Subjectivity, Class, and Gender."

3. Habermas famously described the bourgeois public sphere as "the sphere of private people come together as a public; they soon claimed the public sphere regulated from above against the public authorities themselves, to engage them in a debate over the general rules governing relations in the basically privatized but publicly relevant sphere of commodity exchange and social labor" (27).

Chapter 6
"The War for the Word Has Begun"[1]

And I recount this story to you, not to divert you and take away from the time you need to look at all the things that you have to look at in this meeting. No. I'm telling it to you because this story that comes from so far away reminds us that it is through thinking and feeling comes the light that helps us to seek. With heart and head we must be bridges, so that the men and women of all the worlds may walk from night to day. (Marcos 369)

What we are telling you happened long, long ago, that is, today. (Marcos 389)

[T]o live is to live a life politically, in relation to power, in relation to others, in the act of assuming responsibility for a collective future. To assume responsibility for a future, however, is not to know its directions fully in advance, since the future, especially the future with and for others, requires a certain openness and unknowingness; it implies becoming part of a process the outcomes of which no one subject can surely predict. It also implies that a certain agonism and contestation over the course of direction will and must be in play. Democracy does not speak in unison; its tunes are dissonant, and necessarily so. It is not a predictable process; it must be undergone, like a passion must be undergone. It may also be that life itself becomes foreclosed when the right way is decided in advance, when we impose what is right for everyone and without finding a way to enter into community, and to discover there the "right" in the midst of cultural translation. It may be that what is right and what is good consist in staying open to the tensions that beset the most fundamental categories we require, in knowing unknowingness at the core of what we know, and what we need, and in recognizing the sign

of life in what we undergo without certainty about what will come.
(Butler, *Undoing Gender*, 39)

The war for the word has begun. (Marcos)

Introduction

In this book, our objective has been to develop pedagogical praxis that emerges
from a culture studies tradition and rhetorical tradition, undertaken with the
possibility, as the quotation from Judith Butler suggests, of offering situated
examples of pedagogical strategies and practices. These strategies and practices
suggest a response to the current moment that "assume[s] responsibility for a
future," as we "do not know its direction fully in advance" (Butler, *Undoing
Gender*, 39).[2] Throughout the book we have asked several questions that we see
as important to ask at this conjutural moment: How can pedagogy be
conceptualized so we see it as a site to intervene in culture and to act politically,
emerging from cultural sites and agents who respond democratically to
particular historical moments? How do we develop the desire and habit to
recognize moments when we move beyond norms and develop new ways of
seeing, acting, and relating? How do we see activism not as an end in itself but
as an integral process of revitalizing democracy? This chapter finds points of
convergence between libratory academic intellectual traditions and the
embedded knowledge of political communities in activist struggle, specifically
the Zapatistas of Chiapas, Mexico.

Neoliberalism, a collection of political economic theories and practices,
is also a "strong" rhetoric, an educational force of culture that shapes peoples
and practices. In this sense, neoliberalism is a pedagogy that channels how we
envision and practice democracy. What is hegemonic about neoliberalism is not
just its economic policies and practices but its particular rhetorical construction
of democracy. Democracy, at this conjucture, is a particular discourse and set of
practices which have authority and have been successful in building alliances
among a range of social actors and nation-states.[3] This specific discourse and
practice of democracy is, in part, what enables neoliberalism to be hegemonic. It
has decided in advance what democracy looks like and there is a consensus,
rhetorical and otherwise, to this hegemon.[4]

Throughout the book, we have suggested a rewriting of pedagogy as
rhetorical action. This certainly includes creating and cultivating literacies that
can intervene in neoliberal pedagogy and discourse and move beyond it.
However, we are talking about rhetorical action as more than one's ability to
critique or undo dominant discourses. Rhetorical action refers to practices that
activate excess, including, new literacies that create openness for new
pedagogies, and, as the previous chapter discusses, emergent structures of
feeling that make possible new affective relations and politics. Rhetorical action
includes, as Butler's work suggests, a disruption or rupture of a familiar, or

dominant, discursive terrain in order to create a "certain openness and unknowingness" (39). This work, as we argue, requires a re-articulation of the whole complex of social relations—productive and reproductive labor, structures of feeling, identities, agency, voice, and democratic participation. This complete re-articulation sets the stage for intervention in rhetorical spaces that are fundamental for a democracy to come.[5]

In this final chapter, we identify two rhetorical traditions, one intellectual and mostly situated in universities, and the other, a practice of political communities in activist struggle. Considered in dialogue, these rhetoricians work with language in the interest of pedagogy—pedagogies of and for democracy.[6] These traditions emerge from different locations, but they both situate rhetoric as action, that is, a pedagogical effort that means to create and remake democracy.[7] The academic rhetoricians emerge from a Marxist cultural studies tradition, including academics such as Gayatri Spivak, Raymond Williams, Stuart Hall, Michel Foucault, Judith Butler, Jacques Derrida, and Michael Hardt and Antonio Negri. This rhetoric engages the work that language does and can do in the everyday practices and contemporary conditions of capital. These academic rhetoricians are writing everyday practices of social change through their discussions of language, pedagogy, ethics and philosophy.

The second tradition we are terming a tradition of political-communities-in-struggle. In particular, we see the Zapatistas as offering a new rhetoric, "a wind from below," that challenges a priori claims of authoritative practices, creatively, joyously, and persuasively. In Zapatista writing there is a timely move toward rearticulating the whole complex of social relations.[8] Their rearticulation is not limited to one specific historical moment or discourse. Rather, the Zapatistas rearticulate the web of power over the last 500 years (and beyond). Their rhetoric addresses patriarchy, sexuality, Otherness, colonization, neoliberalism, among other residual and emergent discourses and structures of feeling as the following well known quote from Subcommandante Marcos suggests:

> Majority-which-disguises-itself-as-untolerated-minority P.S.: About this whole thing about whether Marocs is homosexual: Marcos is gay in San Francisco, black in South Africa, Asian in Europe, Chicano in San Isdro, Anarchist in Spain, Palestinian in Israel, Indigenous in the streets of San Cristobal, bad boy in Neza, rocker in CU, Jew in Germany, ombudsman in the SEDENA, feminist in political parties, Communist in the post-Cold War era, prisoner in Cintalapa, pacifist in Bosnia, Mapuche in the Andes, teacher in the CNTE, artist without a gallery or portfolio, housewife on any given Saturday night in any neighborhood of any city of any Mexico, guerrillero in Mexico at the end of the twentieth century, striker in the CTM, reporter assigned to filler stories for the back pages, sexist in the feminist movement, woman alone in the metro at 10 p.m., retired person in planton in the Zocalo, campesino without land, fringe editor, unemployed worker, doctor without a practice, rebellious student, dissident in neoliberalism, writer without books or readers, and, to be sure, Zapatista

in the Mexican Southeast. In sum, Marcos is a human being, any human
being, in this world. Marcos is all minorities who are untolerated,
oppressed, resisting, exploding, saying "Enough!" (Marcos 214)

Bringing these rhetoricians—academic and political-communities-in-struggle—
together enables us to understand social and political formations, to explain and
disrupt these formations, and in so doing, create pedagogies for an openness and
unknowingness, a democracy to come. We should emphasize the point our
colleague, Randi Kristensen makes, that the move to pair, *to put in dialogue*,
these two rhetorics we are not interested in subsuming Zapatista and the
rhetorics of "other" political-communities-in-struggle under an *academic*
discourse of cultural studies. That move, as Kristensen aptly points out, moves a
critique of race from the center of rhetorical action and subsumes the radical
critique of race into an academic discourse—a move all too familiar to political-
communities-in-struggle around the globe. The move to put these rhetoricians in
dialogue is to both enact the vision of a democracy, a "future with and for
others" (Butler 39) in order to "open a crack in history (Marcos 216), and
"staying open to the tensions that beset the most fundamental categories we
require" (Butler 39). Or as Marcos writes, "what we are telling you happened
long, long ago, that is, today" (Marcos 389).

The traditional organization of knowledge production positions, say,
Gayatri Spivak and the Zapatistas in two different rhetorical traditions, i.e.
academic, institutional, First World, and the center of global capital, or, social
movements, Third World, and the "margins" of capital. We suggest that these
rhetors are engaged in a similar political/rhetorical project.

First is language of and for timely political, democratic action: *kairos*,
rhetorical timeliness or timely rhetorical action, democracy to come. Both the
academic and political-communities-in-struggle rhetorics are *sophistic*, in Susan
Jarratt's understanding, insofar as they are working to determine the available
means of effective intervention. They "write," in a particular time and in a
particular space, in response to a particular cultural moment, and as part of a
particular historical phase or crisis of that phase. To use the language of cultural
studies, their writing is embedded in a particular conjucture.[9] Or, to use the
language of the Zapatistas, "this story that comes from so far away reminds us
that it is through thinking and feeling comes the light that helps us to seek"
(Marcos 369). These rhetors are creative in responding to the moment, as
Carolyn Miller says, their ". . . action [s](rhetorical or otherwise) . . . will be
understood as uniquely meaningful within those circumstances" (xiii). "With
heart and head we must be bridges," Marcos joins, "so that the men and women
of all the worlds may walk from night to day" (369).

We also suggest that these rhetors are engaged in what Gayatri Spivak
calls *teleopoiesis*: the imaginative act of moving outside of ourselves, without
guarantees, which does not assume immediate contact or translatability (*Death
of a Discipline*, 31 and 110).[10] Spivak distinguishes *poiesis*—a term from
Aristotle which means imaginative making—from *teleopoiesis*, Derrida's word

in *Politics of Friendship* that emphasizes the unverifiability of this imaginative making. This imaginative gesture, without guarantees, is one that Spivak uses to direct her work towards activist networks of affiliation and communities outside the academy, the movement of "learning to learn from below" (36). Spivak's work situates rhetorical action as a "practical philosophy," a pedagogy, that "trains its current teachers in the habits of democratic reflexes" (36). We can see this kind of move to "learn from below" in Marcos's character, Don Durito of the Lacondon—a beetle—from which Marcos is continuously learning, a process that would otherwise be ignored by authorized discursive traditions.

Viewed as *kairotic* writing, neither the Zapatistas nor the cultural studies scholars are "doing philosophy." Rather, they are exploring and opening spaces for political intervention and possibility, a movement to "stage the question of collectivity" (Spivak 26), or *teleopoiesis*. That is not to say, that every act of writing (or reading) is by itself a political action—if we are to understand political action as an overt act of persuasion or resistance against a hegemonic order. However, these actions open possibilities in the moment, offering opportunities for rearticulating "settled" issues in new ways (Poulakos 95). As Byron Hawk has argued, in order for ethical, political action to take place, it is necessary first to have access to all of the available means of persuasion. Drawing from Spinoza's theory of ethics, Hawk defines ethical action as "increasing the range of action and movement of those in your communicative networks." By contrast, unethical political action reduces the actions of movements of those in your communicative networks. So, for example, propaganda, while "rhetorical" and "persuasive," is unethical in that it eliminates alternative possibilities and reduces the actions of its intended recipients to a very narrow range (Hawk), that is, the neoliberal concept of democracy.

This is not to say that deconstruction or analysis of texts accomplishes this work in and of itself (as many of the critics of deconstruction want to make it). However, the act of creating openings in the fabric of a seemingly settled hegemony—a disruption of the familiar or dominant discursive terrain, a gesture to openness and unknowingness—is a key political action that is an integral aspect for producing even the possibility of counter-hegemonic action. In this sense, the rhetorics and rhetors we are discussing are engaged in "performative acts" that are productive. That is, cultural activity as political activism, or political action as cultural activity (Wright 35). These actions are not necessarily aimed at the "State" or multinational corporations. They are about creating political communities, "staging of collectivities," that rearticulate networks of affinity.

What separates their interventions is their *location in relation to capital*—spatially, historically, institutionally, and in terms of class. Here we are talking specifically about class as suggested by David Harvey and other critical geographers constituting a collective across difference. That is, not simply a working class that is produced by its relationship to labor, but class as it is produced across and through discourses of difference, of difference in power. In terms of cultural studies and Zapatista rhetorics, we do not approach them as different "levels" of discourse. Rather, we are bringing them in dialogue in order to argue that rhetorical actions are concrete, historical, cultural, political, material, social, and productive in the manner and form of their presentation. The Zapatistas and the cultural studies rhetors we have discussed are clearly "different"—both from each other and from the traditions within which they are rooted. The Zapatistas are rooted in traditions of guerilla armies, liberation struggles, postcolonialism, neoliberalism, indigenous struggle, and the State apparatus. All of these traditions are in play in the Zapatistas' context.[11]

However, they creatively produce alternatives through their practices in ways that rearticulate their actions into new possibilities. For example, the Zapatistas clearly differentiate themselves from past guerilla movements, but do not dismiss those movements.[12] They are a "guerilla movement" that does not want to attack or replace the State. They seem to resemble past guerilla movements insofar as they are clad in military gear, have their headquarters in the mountains, and have used guerilla tactics in their military operations. However, the Zapatistas also seem to complicate the dominant narrative about guerilla armies. They do not seek to take control of state power by force and they seek to constantly de-center leadership (Marcos is a SUB-commandante; sometimes when the Zapatistas are in negotiation with the government, Marcos will remain, literally, outside). Not to mention that their most recognizable leader writes stories about discussions with his beetle and posts them to the Internet.

Likewise, cultural studies academics are located within the Western dominated university system.[13] They are rooted in traditions of disciplinarity, canons, nationalism, pedagogy, pluralism, ideas, and intellectual work as academic training. There are also long traditions of radical scholarship and activism and attempts to expand access to knowledge, literacy, and democracy. All of these traditions are also in play as part of the the contexts of cultural studies academics. However, they also, like the Zapatistas, creatively produce alternatives through their practices in ways that rearticulate their actions into new rhetorical and political possibilities. In this sense, it should not be a surprise that cultural studies academics have sought to refigure the relationship between the academy and "the streets," to "cross and trouble boundaries" among disciplines, challenging the compartmentalization of knowledge, and resisting the form and contents of academic writing and performance.[14] Both the Zapatistas and cultural studies academics make choices within and against these contexts in response to particular cultural moments, historical phases, or (sustained) crisis of capital to create alternatives. Neither makes claims to be completely free or outside of its historical contexts. Yet, each reworks and remakes its contexts in order to open new possibilities and to *create* counter-hegemonic spaces through rhetorical action.

John Trimbur has argued that compositionists have tended to "equate the activity of composing with writing itself and miss altogether the complex delivery systems through which writing circulates" thereby isolating "writing from the material conditions of production" ("Composition," 189–90).[15] What we wish to emphasize here is that it is crucial to pay attention to how the concrete situation affects the mode of discourse, or the expression of rhetorical inquiry. That is, to understand and inquire into the political work a group of scholars or political communities does, requires us to think carefully about the ways in which the "writer" is situated within a material history, a specific social formation that determines, in part, the kinds of openings possible and desireable, Isolating writing from their material circumstances would force us to treat any act of political discourse as an expression of a standardized model of language use, thereby erasing not only the conditions of production, but the rhetors themselves. That is, to hold Zapatista rhetoric up to the same generic standards as post-structuralist theorists, or vice versa, forces us to flatten the social field and take people out of their histories and locations.

Such a flattening would also force us to read all rhetorical productions only on a surface level. That is, putting a Zapatista text next to an academic cultural studies text, we would only be able to see them in their absolute difference. They would amount to, simply, two distinct "genres" of text that are not, and perhaps cannot, be in dialogue. This would reinforce an issue that Hardt and Negri discuss in *Empire*: that differently located political movements and discourses "appear from the beginning to be already old and outdated—precisely because they cannot communicate, because their languages cannot be translated" (*Empire*, 56).

But Hardt and Negri do not succumb to despair at the appearance of this inability to communicate. The fact that the discourse of cultural studies "cannot be translated" into the discourse of the Zapatistas without a significant loss of meaning and urgency is no different than the ways in which today political movements around the world cannot be reduced to a single slogan or political banner. Hardt and Negri seem to be updating the language of Marx's *Eighteenth Brumaire* in which Marx sought to account for *how* radical political movements articulate and narrate their struggles. Marx writes,

> Men make their own history, but they do not make it just at they please; they do not make it under circumstances chosen by themselves, but under circumstances directly encountered and transmitted from the past. The tradition of all the dead generations weighs like a nightmare on the brain of the living. And just when they seem engaged in revolutionizing themselves and things, in creating something that has never yet existed, precisely in such periods of revolutionary crisis they anxiously conjure up the spirits of the past to their service and borrow from them names, battle cries and costumes in order to present the new scene of world history. (*Eighteenth*, 15)

The fact that people make history out of conditions not chosen by themselves, merely underscores the importance of history and the rhetorical/cultural contexts within which political work takes place. Ignoring the context, or seeking to reduce all political discourse to a singular genre, would amount to ignoring the fact that *people-in-history* make history and their resultant modes of discourse will reflect their historical situatedness. Hardt and Negri seem to have a similar assumption in mind as they look to the emergent struggles in and against Empire. They argue:

> We can certainly recognize real obstacles that block the communication of struggles. One such obstacle is the absence of a recognition of a common enemy against which the struggles are directed. Beijing, Los Angelos, Nablus, Chiapas, Paris, Seoul; the situations all seem utterly particular. But in fact they all directly attack the global order of empire and seek a real alternative. Clarifying the nature of the common enemy is thus an essential political task. A second obstacle, which is really a corollary to the first, is that there is no common language of struggles that could "translate" the particular language of each into a cosmopolitan language. Struggles in other parts of the world and even our own struggles seem to be written in an incomprehensible foreign language. This too points toward an important political task: to construct a new common language that facilitates communication, as the languages of anti-imperialism and proletarian internationalism did for the struggles of the previous era. Perhaps this needs to be a new type of communication that functions not on the basis of resemblances but on the basis of differences: a communication of singularities. (56–57)

As they call for a new type of communication, Hardt and Negri also hold the possibility that the goal is not necessarily the creation of the new universal language or an international revolution of a reconstituted proletariat. Because the "common enemy" is no longer in the center of Empire—it is deterritorialized across the globe—these local movements, which do not wait "for any sort of external aid or extension to guarantee their effectiveness," can leap vertically—not horizontally—directly into the "virtual center of Empire" (58).

Hardt and Negri's move beyond a universal language takes us back to our discussions of democracy. The goal is not to link everyone in one united struggle—if by "united" we mean same, or singular, in all locations regardless of context. While there is not a need for singular struggle, this does not get rid of the need of a praxis for democracy-in-difference. Where the goals of the revolutionary movements of the past was to extend the revolutionary model so it could be reproduced in other locations throughout the globe, paying only cursory attention to local differences, the democratic project and the need for a language of democracy-in-difference is that communication across differences is a collective, pedagogical experience. If in a liberal democracy people come to a forum to make a decision that will be common to all, a democracy-in-difference—a democracy to come—would be a coming together to exchange, to learn, to expand, the available means of political/rhetorical action. It makes sense in this context, then, the shared project for cultural studies academics and political-communities-in-struggle of thinking through the politics and practice of communicating *in* difference.

We've argued from the beginning of this book that pedagogy emerges from alternative cultural sites and agents; and, universities are not the sole proprietors of pedagogy or knowledge. We have asked about the conditions in which we can be responsive to these pedagogical possibilities that lie outside the university (the A-16 IMF/World Bank protests were one example) and to recuperate democratic traditions that emerge from within the university. We continue to ask: how can we create moments to process new arguments, respond to particular conjunctures, and create new languages that articulate the contingencies and affinities of the particular moment? Our objective is to initiate a dialogue between cultural studies scholarship and political-communities-in-struggle because, as we have argued, effective political struggle, social identities, rhetorics, and structures of feeling emerge only in relation to each other. For those of us situated in universities, these articulations enable us to think about the historical and contemporary traditions of struggle that we can learn from so that our teaching—broadly conceived—can be not just relevant to but actively participate in "learning from below."

Rupture, Rhetoric, and Political Action: A Zapatista Example

On January 14, 1994, the day that NAFTA was implemented, in Chiapas, Mexico—an impoverished state in the Mexican southeast—the Zapatista Army for National Liberation rose up in arms against the Mexican government. The armed rebellion lasted twelve days, but, in a gesture that asks us to rethink the meaning of violence and rebellion, the Zapatistas renounced the traditional revolutionary call to seize state power and willingly withdrew from the towns they had captured back into the mountains of the Mexican Southeast. From the jungle, the Zapatistas started *writing* as a means of creating political community and creating a political voice. Zapatista writing, as we will go on to explain, was at once rhetorical (to determine the available means for effective action) and political: rhetorical action as political action, and political action as rhetorical.

Voicing their opposition through written communiqués that they distribute to the world via the Internet, the Zapatistas critique the corrupt practices and officials of the Mexican government, particularly their ties to global capital, as well as the structures, policies, discourses, pedagogies, and affects of a neoliberal system, a system which they argue has been in place for over five hundred years. Yet most significantly, their struggle "leaps immediately to the global level and attacks the imperial constitution in its generality" (Hardt and Negri, *Empire*, 56). Their communiqués make the move to attack global capital in its generality (the authoritative discourse that runs through patriarchy, sexuality, Otherness, colonization, neoliberalism, among other residual and emergent discourses and structures of feeling) and to create rhetorical action: disrupture of familiar or dominant discursive terrain, that suggests, asserts, and persuades that another world is possible.

As an example, in a communiqué entitled "The Story of the Tiny Mouse and the Tiny Cat," written in August of 1995, just after the armed uprising, Marcos tells a story that becomes an allegory for the Zapatista rebellion in the context of neoliberalism:

> DON DURITO OF THE LACANDON, knight-errant, the undoer of wrongs, the ladies' restless dream, the young men's aspiration, the last and grandest of that exemplary race that made humanity great with such colossal and selfless feats, the beetle and warrior of the moon, writes to you.
>
> I have commanded my loyal squire, the one you call "Sup Marcos," to send you a greeting in writing with all the requirements fit for today's diplomacy, excluding the rapid-intervention forces, the economic programs and the flight of capital. Nevertheless, I want to write you some lines with the sole intent the spirit, to fill your minds with good and noble thoughts. That is why I send you the following tale, full of rich and varying feats. The story forms part of the collection *Stories for a Night of Asphyxiation* (which will probably not be published in the near future).

> The Story of the Tiny Mouse and the Tiny Cat

> THERE ONCE WAS A TINY mouse who was very hungry and wanted to eat a tiny bit of cheese, which was in the tiny kitchen of a tiny house. Very decidedly, the tiny mouse went to the tiny kitchen to grab the tiny bit of cheese. But, it so happened that a tiny cat crossed his path, and the tiny mouse became very frightened and ran away and was not able to get the tiny bit of cheese from the tiny kitchen. Then the tiny mouse was thinking of what to do to get the tiny bit of cheese from the tiny kitchen and he thought and he said:
> "I know. I am going to put out a small plate with a little milk and the tiny cat is going to start drinking the milk because tiny cats like very much a little milk. And then, when the tiny cat is drinking the tiny milk and is not paying attention, I am going to the tiny kitchen to grab the tiny bit of cheese and I am going to eat it. That's a *veeery* good idea," said the tiny mouse to himself.
> And then he went to look for the milk, but it turns out that the milk was in the tiny kitchen, and when the tiny mouse wanted to go to the tiny kitchen, the tiny cat crossed his path and the tiny mouse was very frightened and could not get the milk. Then the tiny mouse was thinking of what to do to get the milk in the tiny kitchen and he thought and he said:
> "I know. I am going to toss a tiny fish very far away and then the tiny cat is going to run to go eat the tiny fish, because tiny cats like very much tiny fish. And then, when the tiny cat is eating the tiny fish and is not paying attention, I'm going to go to the tiny kitchen to grab the tiny bit of cheese and I'm going to eat it. That's a *veeery* good idea," said the tiny mouse.

Then he went to look for the tiny fish, but it happened that the tiny fish was in the tiny kitchen, and when the tiny mouse wanted to go to the tiny kitchen, the tiny cat crossed his path and the tiny mouse became very frightened and ran away and could not go to get the tiny fish.

And then the tiny mouse saw that the tiny bit of cheese, the milk, and the tiny fish, everything that he wanted, was in the tiny kitchen, and he could not get there because the tiny cat would not allow it. And then the tiny mouse said; "Enough!" and he grabbed a machine gun and shot the tiny cat, and he went to the tiny kitchen and he saw that the tiny fish, the milk, and the tiny bit cheese had gone bad and could not be eaten. So he returned to where the tiny cat was, cut it in pieces, and made a great roast. Then, he invited all his friends, and they partied and ate the roasted tiny cat, and they sang and danced and lived very happily. And once there was . . .

This is the end of the story and the end of this missive. I want to remind you that the divisions between countries only serve to illustrate the crime of "contraband" and to give sense to war. Clearly, there exist at least two things greater than borders: one is the crime disguised as modernity, which distributes misery on a world scale; the other is the hope that shame exists only when one fumbles a dance step, and not every time we look in the mirror. To end the first and to make the second one flourish, we need only to struggle to be better. The rest follows of its own accord, and is what usually fills libraries and museums.

It is not necessary to conquer the world, it is sufficient to make it anew . . .

Vale. Health to you, and know that a bed is only a pretext for love; that a tune is only an adornment to dance; and that nationalism is merely a circumstantial accident for struggle.

From the mountains of the Mexican Southeast
DON DURITO OF THE LACANDON

P.S.
PLEASE EXCUSE THE BREVITY of these letters. It so happens that I must press ahead with my expedition to invade Europe this winter. How do you feel about a landing next January 1? (309)

There are two things about "The Story of the Tiny Mouse and the Tiny Cat" that we want to point out. [16] First, that while this allegory can be read as being directed to and about the indigenous Mexican people, and is rooted in local conditions, it also goes to the heart of Empire (read: to end the first [modernity] and make the second [dancing] flourish we need only to struggle to be better). Second, the rhetoric of this allegory—its "silliness," its humor, its simplicity— and the affective relations that it creates is what makes the intervention into Empire possible (read: "It so happens that I must press ahead with my expedition to invade Europe this winter"). This is a reversal of the colonialist enterprise through writing, opening the writing into difference. The rhetoric *itself* is action.

In "The Tiny Mouse and the Tiny Cat," Marcos gives us irrationality, play, silliness, and laughter *as a radical discourse of resistance and action*. That is, this allegory is *veeery* "serious" insofar as it is offered as a public explanation of the Zapatistas' military incursion into San Cristobal. Its seriousness comes out of specific material, political, and cultural conjunctures, not from a specific discursive or political genre.

In Zapatista writing, the transgression of authoritative rhetoric through laughter has the effect of creating informal, discursive space where different identities, positions, and voices come together. We hear, in the laughter and humor, difference, the possibility of different discourses, different meanings, and different ways of being. As the laughter merges the emotional and philosophical and the political, it speaks to how we think and how we feel, what we think and feel about, and possibilities for thinking that are also about the possibilities for feeling.[17] This discourse creates new ideas of community and participation by civil society.[18] As Marcos argues:

> It is not just the Zapatistas who are fighters of resistance. There are many groups (and there are several gathered here) who have also made a weapon of resistance, and they are using it. There are indigenous, there are workers, there are women, there are gays, there are lesbians, there are students, there are young people. Above all there are young people, men and women who name their own identities: "punk," "ska," "goth," "metal," "trasher," "rapper," "hip-hopper," and "etceteras." If we look at what we have in common, that we are "other" and "different." Not only that, we also have in common that we are fighting in order to continue being "other" and "different," and that is why we are resisting. And to those in power, we are "other" and "different;" in other words, we are not like they want us to be, but what we are. (168)

In this example, Marcos underscores the principle of difference as central to the kind of "other" world they are working for. The *Encuentro* was a moment of concrete envisioning, a shift from a reliance on an established center of power to future interventions and possibilities (Miller xiii). As José Rabasa suggests, Zapatista discourse creates "a political space where different positions may confront each other rather than a pluralistic centrist position" (565).

The effect of Marcos's laughter is simultaneously joyous, transgressive, and renewing. As Bakhtin suggests, laughter and humor, *reveal* discourse as authoritative. He argues further that the "authoritative word is located in a distanced zone, organically connected with a past that is felt to be hierarchically higher . . . it is therefore not a question of choosing it from among other possible discourses that are its equal" (*Dialogic Imagination*, 342). At the core of Bakhtin's analysis is the discursivity of language:

no living word relates to its object in a singular way: between the word and its object, between the word and the speaking subject, there exists an elastic environment of other, alien words about the same object, the same theme, and this is an environment that is often difficult to penetrate. It is precisely in the process of living interaction with this specific environment that the word may be individualized and given stylistic shape. (*Dialogic Imagination*, 276)

In other words, if laughter suggests that there are other discourses available, that an authoritative discourse is not *a priori* given, but constructed, other meanings can fill our thoughts and emotions. The humor, by suggesting other words and other meanings, suggests change and renewal. This change and renewal disrupts both the bourgeois narrative and the stogginess of much anti-neoliberal, leftist critique.

When Marcos asks us to excuse the brevity of his letters because "I must press ahead with my expedition to invade Europe this winter," we hear absurdity, joy, and an assertion of change to come. The transgression emerges from the humor that breaks boundaries of authoritative discourse with its "sense of the gay relativity of prevailing truths and authorities" (Bakhtin, *Rabelais*, 11). This is the Zapatista's "war for the word": it is the recuperation of laughter in the face of authoritative discourse that poses a serious challenge to the hegemony of this discourse.[19]

Marcos's laughter has simultaneously an emotional and philosophical impact. It engages our feelings and thoughts about the social world. As Williams says about structures of feelings, it works with "meanings and values as they are actively lived and felt" but are simultaneously social *and* personal experiences. Laughter is a way of thinking, living, and understanding that is simultaneously personal, local, and social, and even universal. Rhetorical action activates and creates links between differently situated people, connecting individuals to collective experiences.

When Judith Butler writes that democracy does not have a singular voice or meaning, her philosophical prose suggests the possibility of laughter as a philosophy. If we argue with Butler that "democracy does not speak in unison; its tunes are dissonant, and necessarily so," we can include within dissonant sounds of democracy, the laughter, humor, and transgression of Zapatista writing. This humor and laughter, to go back to Bakhtin, is emotion that has "deep philosophical meaning" (66).

We argue, therefore, that the emotional and philosophical meaning of laughter in Marcos's story is a *rhetorical action* and *affective action* for democracy, a democracy to come. As it uses humor, Zapatista rhetoric claims, or reclaims, the discourse of freedom, dignity, and rights that neoliberalism (and other discourses of capitalism) lays claim to. What the Zapatistas clearly point out is that neoliberal ideas about freedom, rights, and democracy are for the bourgeois, for the nation-state, and for capital. They are not universal ideals as the discourse claims. In a world where it can be claimed that democracy for a few is democracy for everyone, the tiny mouse (the Zapatistas) engages in a "war for the word" that challenges the authority, contradictions, and universality of the tiny cat (neoliberal discourse). In so doing, Zapatista rhetoric imagines identities, voices, and political spaces that are not bound up with the logic of capitalism. Their writing calls forth a new world, rhetorical action that imagines a world that is exterior to capitalism (Rabasa 577).[20]

The allegory comes out of the conjunctures of the material, political, and cultural conditions of Mexico at the moment of a global trade pact that fuses the past, present, and future of the indigenous in Mexico to the global neoliberal order. But as Hardt and Nergi argue, these political, social, and economic relations are consistent with Empire's logic. The Zapatistas' allegory, then, extends well beyond a nationalist critique—it is at once an allegory about Empire that offers a connective rhetorical praxis of resisting Empire and presenting a glimpse of a democracy to come.

When the tiny mouse shoots the tiny cat and has a big party, we respond to the silliness of the narrative but hear the more serious suggestion that violence has a place in the face of oppression. But we also hear the tragedy and violence of everyday life and violence as a necessary response. The abundance of food that was just beyond the reach of the mouse had "gone bad," had been wasted. The disturbing image of the cat being cut up and roasted for a party with all the other mice, *could have been avoided*, and was never the goal of the mice. Violence here was a last resort for survival, and even then the mouse found the means of survival had been left to spoil, feeding no one. The mice are forced to *become the cat*, become carnivores, out of necessity. This allegory explains the moment of intervention, and violence, and at the same time offers strategy for moving beyond this situation.

When Marcos ends the communiqué with "a bed is only a pretext for love; that a tune is only an adornment to dance; and that nationalism is merely a circumstantial accident for struggle," the emphasis is on "love, dance, and struggle" not the particular forms these take. Love, dance, and struggle are about modes of life that are sustainable, that are about relations among equals, and that are intertwined with affective difference. If this narrative were a national liberation movement narrative and not a Zapatista narrative, the Nation and nationalism would be the ONLY form through which resistance could be expressed. But from a Zapatista position, since the Nation is not the "origin" of exploitative social relations, it is but an "accident" of the moment. What is "permanent" are the creative energies of the multitude (love, dance, struggle), not the particular forms (bed, tune, nation). The Zapatistas are also offering a critique of national liberation movements as an effective form of revolutionary movement in Empire. While they invoke Che Guevara, they move beyond nationalist discourse that he has come to symbolize. While their appearance first took a familiar form of a national liberation struggle (armed guerilla groups taking over a town), they quickly refused the narrative and political practice of a "guerilla war" by returning to the mountains of the Mexican Southeast to write and to organize.

Marcos ends the story of the tiny mouse and the tiny cat with the beginning of another narrative: "and once there was . . . ". Marcos is suggesting the story is leading elsewhere, to other stories, other narratives, to other forms of writing, and to other pedagogical moments. It ends by not knowing in advance the precise form of the language, rhetoric, and democracy to come. It is an "ending" that is a beginning. "To assume responsibility for a future," Judith Butler argues, "is not to know its directions fully in advance, since the future, especially the future with and for others, requires a certain openness and unknowingness; it implies becoming part of a process the outcomes of which no one subject can surely predict" (39).

In this communiqué and others like it, Marcos deliberately plays with the borders, boundaries of authoritarian discourse, making fun of it, suggesting silliness and mocking its seriousness, and leaving open a space for difference, for others. His unknowingness, his partially begun "next story," is a commitment to a future with and for others. In his discussion of constituent power, Antonio Negri similarly describes such a commitment to a future: "we are interested in a hermeneutics that, beyond words and through them, can grasp the life, the alternatives, the crisis and recomposition, the construction and the creation of a faculty of humankind: a faculty to construct a political arrangement" (Negri, *Insurgencies*, 35). It is the creation of this rhetoric and structures of feeling that marks the revolutionary activity and pedagogical possibilities: these are specific conjunctural responses that create conditions for organic movements. Zapatista writing is more than a critique of neoliberalism. It is "a wind from below," that creates new democratic possibilities.

Their rhetoric articulates, what Kenneth Burke calls "strategies for the encompassing of situations," articulating a new social and political force (qtd. in Clifford, *Writing Culture*, 11). The Zapatistas seize language for situated rhetorical and political action. Their words become a political force, a mode of action in the world that creates communities, solidarities, and political strategies.[21]

Rhetorical Action: Academic Work

To extend this discussion of rhetorical action into a discussion of pedagogy for democracy, we return to the contexts with which we opened the book. Neoliberalism, we argued in the first chapter, reflects a shift in values away from questions of democratic deliberation and participation to a focus on the production of workers and consumers for the newest phase of the capitalist economy. This focus also carries with it a peculiar understanding of democracy that is divorced from a practice of democracy as mass participation in self-governance and seeks to eliminate the kind of democratic praxis we address at the beginning of this chapter. We have argued that neoliberalism is a stage of capitalism in which intellectual, material, communicative, and affective labor is produced as surplus value. However, we are not just interested in an analysis or a critique of neoliberalism but in possibilities for alternative practices that such a critique might suggest.[22]

To begin our discussion of the possibilities for alternative practices, we turn, again, to the work of Hardt and Negri who argue that in the current conjuncture, there is a "dynamic and creative relationship between material and social production" (*Empire*, 29). For Hardt and Negri, material and social reproduction is both the site of exploitation and the site of excess that capital cannot contain. This excess is immaterial; that is, it produces subjectivities, identities, and affects that have revolutionary potential. For Hardt and Negri, these emergent subjectivities and affects contain the potential for revolution, but a revolution that exceeds "traditional" understandings of revolutionary organization, strategy, and tactics.[23]

While it may be clear from our discussion how the Zapatistas actively construct timely rhetorical action, it may not be as apparent how cultural studies scholars *produce* new literacies, an openness for new practices and structures of feeling, and in so doing set the stage for a new materialist rhetoric. In fact, many of these scholars have been read primarily as doing the work of re-articulation, breaking down narratives, claims, and held truths, while offering nothing in their place. For example, deconstruction, especially given its location in academia is seen as anti-productive, removed (in the ivory tower), and disconnected from the world.[24] However, we would argue that some cultural studies scholars who are traditionally lumped into this category are not simply engaged in negative critique. Rather, they are engaged in rhetorical action—re-articulation of the whole complex of social relations that set the stage for a new materialist rhetoric—that is specific to the traditions and practices of the academy and the production of knowledge more generally. Yes, it is true that some of this work may be difficult; however, we would argue that part of the difficulty lies in its breaking out of a particular hegemony and rhetoric for how scholarly discourse is articulated.

This political work by cultural studies scholars is misunderstood as elitist and is simultaneously under attack by neoliberalism. Neoliberalism has waged its own war on higher education; it has sought to bring the purpose of higher education under the logic of the market. We have seen increasing attempts to call for "relevance" in research, teaching, and curricula, in which relevance is defined narrowly as relevance for maintaining and expanding markets. Defining relevance in this way, excludes the other purpose of higher education: the preparation of subjects for participating in democracy.

The limiting of the purpose of higher education to the will of capital is certainly not unique to this historical period.[25] What is new is the *particular* form in which capital seeks to bring higher education under its control and the *particular* type of subjects it wants these institutions to produce. We see the work of several cultural studies scholars as engaging in rhetorical action that is at once against the market-based logic of neoliberalism and the control of possible futures, modes of life, and affiliations consistent with traditional

Western-based scholarship. It resists a liberal model of inclusion that has dominated the mainstream of progressive educational policy and rhetorics of diversity. As Robert Mcruer writes:

> "Inclusion" is such a dangerous word, and I would encourage you to generate alternatives to it: resistance, dissent...The communities that I move through—gay or queer communities, communities of people with disabilities, and others—are constantly hearing, these days, about inclusion: neoliberal and corporate boosters have figured out that "including" us is a way to contain us, to dilute our critiques, to transform us into window dressing or entertainment in the world of "happy family multiculturalism" that corporate elites have planned for the future. (Letter to Students)

The cultural studies scholarship that we are reading as rhetorical action for determining the nexus of power/knowledge at a given conjuncture, is explicitly political in that it is a *necessary* task in determining the rhetorical situation and potential for creating openings in (neoliberal) hegemony. The rhetorical and theoretical efforts of this scholarship are directed towards finding excess, gaps, differences, and openings. To move this argument temporarily into Derrida's work, work that explores "*différance*," discursive acts, and the ways in which concepts are open to different meanings, and thus, different possibilities. When a word, a discursive act, or a concept enters culture, it becomes opened to *différance*, that is, it is excessive of its origins, or in Foucault's language, is dislodged from its fixed point in the nexus of power/knowledge. In Derrida's terms, an author cannot control the range of responses by her audience, just as capital cannot control how people relate to its logic. It is our capacity to innovate, to rework, to mock, to imagine, to articulate, to *produce* that is beyond the scope of capital's control. Words, structures of feeling, and labor are excessive of any meaning that is prescribed to them, and thus can become sites of rhetorical action.

For example, in *Undoing Gender*, Butler argues that gender, sexual difference, and humanness can, and need to be, strategically re-appropriated for progressive political use. Like the Zapatistas' rearticulation of a long and complex history of marginalization, oppression, and exclusion, Butler argues for a reworking of hegemonic articulations of gender within and against the specific discourses that reproduce gender marginalization, oppression, and exclusion. This is "not a question merely of producing a new future for genders that do not yet exist," she argues. On the contrary:

> The genders I have in mind have been in existence for a long time, but they have not been admitted into the terms that govern reality. So it is a question of developing within law, psychiatry, social, and literary theory a new legitimating lexicon for the gender complexity that we have been living for a long time. Because the norms governing reality have not

admitted these forms to be real, we will, of necessity, call them "new".
(*Undoing Gender*, 31)[26]

For Butler, the move she is suggesting is not idealist, or "academic," insofar as
the complexity of human existence, particularly the complexity of gender
identities in her example, is not something that is new, nor is it something that
she is constructing out of thin air. The complex articulations of gender *already
exist*, highlighting the excess of gender identities in relation to the "norms
governing reality." Her rhetorical action is a rearticulation, not of the gender
identities themselves (those are already there), but of the terms through which
"reality" is governed. Butler calls for a "critical democratic project," what we
are calling rhetorical action, which requires progressives to "follow a double
path in politics":

> we must use this language [of gender, of "women," of "human"] to assert
> an entitlement to conditions of life in ways that affirm the constitutive role
> of sexuality and gender in political life, and we must also subject our very
> categories to critical scrutiny. We must find the limits of their inclusivity
> and translatability, the presuppositions they include, the ways in which
> they must be expanded, destroyed, or reworked both to encompass and
> open up what it is to be human and gendered. (37–38)

Butler's "double path" of rearticulation highlights the discursive reconstructive
work of rhetorical action. It is not enough to "be against" or to "offer something
new"; it is necessary to rearticulate the network of power/knowledge within and
against the current hegemony. Such work cannot be done in isolation, nor does it
concentrate strictly on the ways in which the State or dominant discourses of
gender position women. Rather, the nexus of power/knowledge implicates the
entire discursive frame and opens a space for its reworking. What is at stake is
which subjects get to lay claim to the real and to the human.

   In summary, the contribution to rhetorical action by these academics is
to identify the particular nexus of power/knowledge, to identify those subjects
who hold power and those who are excluded from power, and finally, to disrupt
the settled meanings, to expose the excess of meaning and possibility in any
discursive system (most significantly, the logic of capital). We call this
rhetorical action, as we have explained, because it is simultaneously *kairotic* and
teleopoietic. That is, it creates a timely opening in dominant discourse and holds
out the possibility of the imaginative act of moving outside of ourselves, without
guarantees that does not assume immediate contact or translatability. In a
context that is increasingly marked by an attempt to bring the production of
knowledge into line with the logic of the market, such an inquiry brings into
focus the specific discursive moves that attempt to articulate education and the
production of knowledge into neoliberalism and makes possible situated action
for a democracy to come.

Notes

1. Subcommandante Marcos, *Our Wordlis Our Weapon.*

2. This concept of pedagogy is tied to Derrida's notion of democracy that we discussed in the first chapter. In Derrida's later work, particularly *Rogues, Negotiations,* and *Politics of Friendship,* democracy is neither a system, government, nor an ideal. Neither is it temporal, something we're working towards in the current structure. It is closely related to Derrida's notion of difference, the impossibility of closing off or deferring meaning in language, the possibility of differentiation or, even opposition (38). As Derrida argues, following Benjamin, "there is not yet any democracy worthy of this name. Democracy *remains* to come: to engender or to regenerate . . . it will always remain to come, it will never be present in the present, it will never present itself, will never come, will remain always to come, like the impossible itself" (82 and 73).

3. See Neil Smith for a discussion of the geography of democracy in the contemporary nation-state.

4. Indeed, at the anti-globalization events, one of mantras of the participants is "*This* is what democracy looks like."

5. Here we're moving beyond Gramsci's call in "The Modern Prince" for strategies and languages that could persuade the masses. Structures of feeling become the sites of strategy.

6. Gayatri Spivak, *Death of a Discipline,* 86. We're mindful, here, of the point our colleague, Randi Kristensen makes, that we do not want to subsume minority rhetorics into the umbrella of cultural studies. That move, as Kristensen aptly points out, moves a critique of race from the center of critical work, and subsumes the radical critique of race into an academic discourse.

7. The Greeks have two notions of time, *chronos* and *Kairos. Chronos* is teleological time, *kairos* is conjunctural time combined with space. It's about the moment. Democracy, in the *kairotic* tradition, has to do with what you make of the here and now. It's not about a promise that you will receive (salvation or heaven); it's about enacting principles of democracy in the particular context, moment, and locality. It's also all those things that lead up to, limiting or opening possibilities, "appropriate time."

8. As Claudia Acuña and Raquel Gutiérrez Aguilar argue in "Social Movements and Progressive Governments: The Current Veins of Latin America," one of the most important ideas that the Zapatistas have given resistance movements is their notion of time: "From these limitations and from the birth of resistance struggles in other Mexican territories, Zapatismo goes on the search for support for a battle that is known to be long, but more and more lonely. The Other Campaign has as its principle merit making visible antagonism," summarizes Raquel. In an election year, with Fox melting like ice under the fire of his own political clumsiness, the horizon saw the arrival of López Obrador, who with a leftist discourse is getting closer to power due to his ability to add on the right. Raquel rescues this jewel that Zapatismo has given to Latin-American resistance: its notion of time. The Other Campaign is more of the same: "we're going to create our own time to put together the cartography of the two Mexicos" (http://www.LaVaca.org/).

9. For a discussion of conjuncture and conjuctural moments, see Gramsci's "The Modern Prince."

10. Also see Spivak's work on translation in her introduction to Mahasweta Devi's *Imaginary Maps*.

11. There are many cultural studies scholars who emerge from activist traditions as well. For a discussion of fields such as Afro-American Studies, Queer Studies, and Women's Studies connections to activism, see Chandra Mohanty's sixth chapter in *Feminism Without Borders*.

12. In 2006, Marcos drove around Mexico on a motorcycle, in a clear invocation of Che Guevara's trip through South America, a trip that politicized Che. Marcos's trip, called the "Other Campaign" is about talking to people, yet his purpose is to create a political movement through civil society, a non-hierarchical movement that moves beyond the state-directed model that Che developed in South America.

13. See our discussion of cultural studies scholars in the introduction for a discussion of how we characterize these intellectual workers.

14. As Randy Martin has discussed, intellectual labor does not just happen in the academy. Universities have claimed intellectual labor as the capital that they produce (degrees) but intellectual labor is clearly in excess of the institution of the University (Martin).

15. He suggests that part of this neglect comes from the "pressures and limits of classroom life and the overdetermined social relations between teachers and students" (189). However, he also argues that part of the problem stems from the "conceptual separation of the canons of rhetoric . . . that has isolated delivery . . . from invention" (189). Trimbur argues that this separation made more sense within ancient Greece where one's audience was present in the polis. However, he argues, in the "democratic revolutions of the modern age, delivery *must* be seen as inseparable from the circulation of writing and widening diffusion of social usefully knowledge" (191). Trimbur's analysis moves to a critique of the "constellated figure of student and teacher *in loco parentis*," which "so thoroughly pervades the study and teaching of writing that it has become commonsensical and unavailable for analysis" (193). This last point is suggestive of a moment of rhetorical action—that is, Trimbur subjects an issue that is seemingly settled (i.e. "commonsensical and unavailable for analysis") to a rhetorical reworking in order to open up alternative possibilities for democratic social movments.

16. For more examples of allegorical communiqués that suggest another future, see Juana Ponce de Leon's collection of Marcos' writing, *Our Word Is Our Weapon*.

17. Here's what Marcos says about Zapatista laughter: "During the peace talks the government delegates have confessed that they have studied hard to learn about dignity and have been unable to understand it. They ask the Zapatista delegates to explain what is dignity. The Zapatistas laugh—after months of pain, they laugh. Their laughter echoes and escapes behind the high wall behind which arrogance hides its fear. The Zapatista delegates laugh even when the dialogue ends, and when they report what has happened. Everyone who hears them laughs, and the laughter recomposes the faces that have been hardened by hunger and betrayal. The Zapatistas laugh in the mountains of the Mexican Southeast, and the sky cannot avoid the contagion of that laughter, and the peals of laughter resound. The laughter is so great that tears well up and it begins to rain, as though laughter were a gift for the dry land" (Marcos, *Our Word Is Our Weapon*, 270).

18. Their appeal, as they declare, is not to "the proletariat as the historical vanguard, but to the civil society that struggles for democracy" (Ponce de Leon, 232).

19. When John Beverley asks, "is it possible to imagine a politics of the Left that is not tied to a telos of modernity," Marcos's humor suggests that the question should

be recast as "is it possible to re-imagine a discourse of the left that is not tied to the discourse of authority?"

20. This is a different move from Paul Gilory's scholarship in *The Black Atlantic* that suggests that those who have been excluded from modernity can fight (literally) for inclusion in its liberatory terms. Zapatista rhetoric as our argument has suggested, creates a hybrid, heterogeneous voice constituted by laughter that challenges an authoritative discourse through its multiplicity. Gilroy "politics of transfiguration therefore reveals the hidden internal fissures in the concept of modernity. The bounds of politics are extended precisely because this tradition refuses to accept that the political is a readily seperable domain. Its basic desire is to conjure up and enact the new modes of friendship, happiness, and solidarity that are consequent on the overcoming of the racial oppression on which modernity and its antinomy of rational, western, progress as excessive barabity relied" (38).

21. See Naomi Klein's article, "Farewell to 'The End of History'," for a discussion of the Zapatistas' influence on the anti-globalization movement.

22. Critique, or critical thinking, is a term that is loosely used in academia. As we've observed in various academic contexts, critical thinking becomes a floating signifier that is untheorized, applied to so many practices that it ceases to be, or it is used to describe practices that, in fact, are not interested in critique at all. Furthermore, in practice, even the most "radical" of critiques carries an assumption about the ends of critique. That is, critique often stops short of considering the question of praxis within particular conjectural moments and the *process* of building and sustaining radical social movements. Often critique assumes an Enlightenment goal of "shedding light" upon a problem in order to expose the "Truth" with the assumption that knowledge of Truth *necessarily* leads to action, or, that "realization" of "Truth" *is* the same thing as revolutionary action. We are not so much interested in proclaiming such goals to be "wrong-headed" or "counter-revolutionary." Rather, we are recognizing a gap in radical political theory that concerns the everyday processes and literacies of political organization and sustaining real people in real movements.

23. Hardt and Negri suggest that "it may be no longer useful to insist on the old distinction between strategy and tactics" (58). Rather, they argue, "the construction of Empire, and the globalization of economic and cultural relationships, means that the virtual center of Empire can be attacked from any point. The tactical preoccupations of the old revolutionary school are thus completely irretrievable; the only strategy available to the struggles is that of a constituent counterpower that emerges from within Empire" (59).

24. As an example, in his review of Gayatri Spivak's *A Critique of Postcolonial Reason*, Terry Eagleton accuses Spivak of unnecessarily and pretentiously difficult language, dull prose, "voguish" guilt-ridden deprecation, and over-seriousness. In his review, Eagleton complains that Spivak's language is awkward, that she is overly concerned with internal questions within the field of postcolonial studies, and that she pays no attention to style, moving within one sentence from one idea to another. In fact, he argues, because she cannot, on the one hand, stick to the point and, on the other hand, because her argument is too narrowly focused, *A Critique of Postcolonial Reason* has no political application outside of her field. Eagleton clearly desires a text that, according to the conventions of academic rhetoric, logically and rationally traces the rhetoric of postcolonial reason. *London Review of Books*, p. 3. See also, Judith Butler's response to Eagleton in the *London Review of Books*, for a critique of Eagleton's position.

25. See Richard Ohmann, *The Politics of Letters*, and James Berlin's *Writing Instruction in 19th Century Colleges*.

26. See Marcos's discussion of the "issue of Marcos's homosexuality" earlier in this chapter.

Works Cited

Acuña, Claudia, and Raquel Gutiérrez Aguilar. "Social Movements and
    Progressive Governments: The Current Veins of Latin America"
    <http://www.LaVaca.org>.
Adorno, Theodore. "The Essay as Form." *New German Critique* 32 (1984): 151–171.
Ahmed, Sara. *The Cultural Politics of Emotion*. New York: Routledge, 2004.
Ang, Ien. "Who Needs Cultural Research?" *CHCI Working Papers*. 1999. CHCI
    Annual Meeting. Brisbane, Australia. <http://www.fas.harvard.edu/
    ~chci/papers.html> 18 July 2006.
Angus, Ian. *Emergent Publics: An Essay on Social Movements and Democracy*.
    Winnipeg, MB: Arbeiter Ring Publishing, 2001.
Aronowitz, Stanley, and Henry Giroux. *Education Still Under Siege*. Westport, CT:
    Bergin and Garvey, 1993.
Bakhtin, M.M. *The Dialogic Imagination: Four Essays*. Ed. Michael Holquist. Austin:
    University of Texas Press, 1981.
———. *Rabelais and His World*. Trans. Helene Iswolsky. Bloomington: Indiana
    University Press, 1984.
Bennett, Tony. *The Birth of the Museum: History, Theory, Politics*. London:
    Routledge, 1995.
Berlant, Lauren. "Introduction: Compassion (and Withholding)." *Compassion: The
    Culture and Politics of an Emotion*. Ed. Lauren Berlant. New York:
    Routledge, 2004.
———. *The Queen of America Goes to Washington City: Essays on Sex and
    Citizenship*. Durham, NC: Duke University Press, 1997.
Berlin, James. *Writing Instruction in 19th Century Colleges*. Carbondale: Southern
    Illinois University Press, 1984.
Beverley, John. "The Im/possibility of Politics: Subalternity, Modernity,
    Hegemony." *The Latin American Studies Reader*. Ed. Ileana Rodriguez.
    Durham, NC: Duke University Press, 2001: 47–63.
Bourdieu, Pierre. *Acts of Resistance: Against the Tyranny of the Market*. New York:
    New Press, 1999.
———. *Firing Back: Against the Tyranny of the Market*. New York: New Press,
    2003.

————. *Outline of a Theory of Practice, An.* Cambridge: Cambridge UP, 1977.

Brown, Danika. "Hegemony and the Discourse of the Land Grant Movement: Historicizing as a Point of Departure." *Journal of Advanced Composition.* 23 (2003): 319–49.

Butler, Brandon. "Criticizing GW Gets Seniors Award." The GW Hatchet/gwhatechet.com. 10 May 2004. <http:// www.gwhatchet.com/media/paper332/news/2004/05/10/ Commencement/Criticizing.Gw.Gets.Seniors.Award-680131.shtml> 27 Dec 2007.

Butler, Judith. "Exacting Solidarities." *London Review of Books.* 1 July 1999. . <http://www.lrb.co.uk/ v21/n13/letters.html> July 2006.

————. *Undoing Gender.* New York: Routledge, 2004.

Butler, Judith and Gayatri Chakrovorty Spivak. *Who Sings The Nation-State: Language, Politics, Belonging.* Calcutta, India: Seagull Books, 2007.

Calhoun, Craig. "Putting Emotions in Their Place." *Passionate Politics: Emotions and Social Movements.* Eds. Jeff Goodwin, Jaspar James, and Francesca Polletta. Chicago: University of Chicago Press, 2001: 47–57.

Chang, Grace. *Disposable Domestics: Immigrant Women Workers in the Global Economy.* Cambridge, MA: South End Press, 2000.

Chomsky, Noam. *Profit Over People: Neoliberalism and Global Order.* New York: Seven Stories Press, 1999.

Chouliaraki, Lilie, and Norman Fairclough. *Discourse in Late Modernity: Rethinking Critical Discourse Analysis.* Edinburgh: Edinburgh University Press, 1999.

Cleaver, Harry. *Reading Capital Politically.* Austin: University of Texas Press, 1979.

Clifford, James. "Introduction: Partial Truths." *Writing Culture: The Poetics and Politics of Ethnography.* Eds. James Clifford and George E. Marcus. Berkeley: University of California Press, 1986: 1–26.

Coogan, David. "The Rhetoric of Reentry." Cultural Studies and Critical Pedagogies for the 21st Century. Summer Symposium. The George Washington University. 10 July 2006. Washington, DC. <http:// mason.gmu.edu/~bhawk/conference/abstracts06.html>.

Cope, Bill, and Mary Kalantizis. *Multiliteracies: Literacy Learning and the Design of Social Futures.* New York: Routledge, 2000.

Cushman, Ellen. *The Struggle and the Tools: Oral and Literate Strategies in an Inner City Community.* Albany, NY: SUNY Press, 1998.

Cvetkovich, Ann. *An Archive of Feeling: Trauma, Sexuality, and Lesbian Public Cultures.* Durham, NC: Duke University Press, 2003.

Dalla Costa, Mariarosa. "Development and Reproduction." *Women, Development, and Labor of Reproduction: Struggles and Movements.* Ed. Mariarosa Dalla Costa and Giovanna F. Dalla Costa. Trenton, NJ: Africa World Press, 1999: 11–45.

Davis, Dawn Rae. "(Love Is) The Ability of Not Knowing: Feminist Experience of the Impossible in Ethical Singularity." *Hypatia.* 17 (2002): 145– 161.

De Man, Paul. *Allegories of Reading: Figural Language in Rousseau, Nietzsche, Rilke, and Proust.* New Haven, CT: Yale University Press, 1979.

Derrida, Jacques. *Negotiations: Interventions, 1971–2001.* Stanford, CA: Stanford University Press, 2002.

————. *Politics of Friendship.* London: New York: Verso, 1997.

————. *Rogues: Two Essays on Reason*. Stanford, CA: Stanford University Press, 2005.

————. "Signature, Event, Context." *A Derrida Reader: Between the Blinds*. Ed. Peggy Kamuf. New York: Columbia University Press, 1991.

————. "Structure, Sign, and Play in the Discourse of the Human Sciences." *Writing and Difference*. Trans. Alan Bass. Chicago: University of Chicago Press, 1978.

Duggan, Lisa. *Twilight of Equality: Neoliberalism, Cultural Politics, and the Attack on Democracy*. Boston: Beacon Press, 2003.

Eagleton, Terry. "In the Gaudy Supermarket." Rev. of *A Critique of Postcolonial Reason*. Gayatri Spivak. *London Review of Books*. 13 May 1999. <http://www.lrb.co.uk/v21/n10/eagl01_.html> July 2006.

Edbauer, Jennifer. "(Meta)Physical Graffiti: 'Getting Up' as Affective Writing Model." *Journal of Advanced Composition*. 25.1 (2005): 131–159.

Ellsworth, Elisabeth. "Why Doesn't this Feel Empowering?: Working Through the Repressive Myths of Critical Pedagogy." *Harvard Educational Review*. 59.3 (1989): 297–324.

Enloe, Cynthia. *Bananas, Beaches, and Bases: Making Feminist Sense of International Politics*. Berkeley: University of California Press, 1990.

Federici, Silvia. "Reproduction and Feminist Struggle in the New International Division of Labor." *Women, Development, and Labor of Reproduction: Struggles and Movements*. Eds. Mariarosa Dalla Costa and Giovanna F Dalla Costa. Trenton, NJ: Africa World Press, 1999: 47–81.

Ferguson, Roderick. *Aberrations in Black: Toward a Queer of Color Critique*. Minneapolis: University of Minnesota Press, 2004.

Foucault, Michel. *The Archeology of Knowledge and The Discourse on Language*. Trans. A.M. Sheridan Smith. New York: Pantheon Books, 1972.

Fraser, Nancy. "Rethinking the Public Sphere: A Contribution to the Critique of Actually Existing Democracy." *Habermas and the Public Sphere*. Ed. Craig Calhoun. Cambridge, MA: MIT Press, 1992: 109–142.

Freire, Paulo. *Education for Critical Consciousness*. New York: Continuum, 1973.

————. *Pedagogy of Hope*. New York: Continuum, 1995.

————. *Pedagogy of the Oppressed*. New York: Continuum, 1970.

Fukuyama, Francis. "After Neoconservatism," *The New York Times Magazine*. 19 Feb. 2006 <http://www.nytimes.com/2006/02/19/magazine/neo.html?ex=1298005200&en=4126fa3 8fefd80de&ei=5090 > 20 July 2006.

————. *America at the Crossroads: Democracy, Power, and the Neoconservative Legacy*. New Haven, CT: Yale UP, 2006.

————. "The End of History?" *The National Interest*. (Summer 1989): 3–18.

————. *The End of History and the Last Man*. New York: Avon Books, 1992.

George, Diana. "A Matter of Life and Death: Public Debate in the Culture of Consent." Conference of College Composition and Communication. Palmer House, Chicago. 25 March 2003.

George Washington University Bulletin, The. Washington, DC: 2003.

Gilroy, Paul. *The Black Atlantic: Modernity and Double Consciousness*. Cambridge, MA: Harvard University Press, 1993.

Giroux, Henry. "Cultural Studies and the Politics of Public Pedagogy: Making the Political More Pedagogical." *Parallax*. 10 (2004): 73–89.

Gramsci, Antonio. *Prison Notebooks*. New York: Columbia University Press, 1992.

Guattari, Félix and Antonio Negri. *Communists Like Us: New Spaces of Liberty, New Lines of Alliance*. New York: Semiotext(e), 1990.

Habermas, Jurgen. *The Structural Transformation of the Public Sphere: An Inquiry into a Category of Bourgeois Society*. Cambridge, MA: MIT Press, 1991.

Hall, Stuart. "Cultural Studies and It's Theoretical Legacies" *Cultural Studies*. Eds. Lawrence Grossberg, Cary Nelson, and Paula Treichler. New York: Routledge, 1992: 277–294.

———. "Culture, the Media and the 'Ideological Effect'" *Mass Communication and Society*. Eds. James Curran, Michael Gurevitch, Janet Woollacott. Beverly Hills and London: Sage Publications, 1977: 315–348.

———. Keynote Address. Cultural Studies Now: An International Conference. University of East London, Docklands Campus, London. 20 July 2007

———. "The Problem of Ideology: Marxism without Guarantees." *Stuart Hall: Critical Dialogues*. Ed. David Morley and Kuan-Hsing Chen. London: Routledge, 1996: 25–46.

———. "Signification, Representation, Ideology: Althusser and the Post-Structuralists Debates." *Critical Studies in Mass Communication*. 2:2 (1985): 91–114.

Hardt, Michael, and Antonio Negri. *Empire*. Cambridge, MA: Harvard University Press, 2000.

———. *Multitude: War and Democracy in the Age of Empire*. New York: The Penguin Press, 2004.

Harvey, David. *A Brief History of Neoliberalism*. Oxford: Oxford University Press, 2005.

———. *The Condition of Postmodernity*. Cambridge, MA: Blackwell, 1990.

———. *Spaces of Global Capitalism: Towards a Theory of Uneven Geographical Development*. London and New York: Verso, 2006.

———. *Spaces of Hope*. Berkeley: University of California Press, 2000.

Hauser, Gerard. *Introduction to Rhetorical Theory*. 2d ed. Prospect Heights, IL: Waveland Press, 2002.

Hawk, Byron. "Extending the Distributed University: Toward a Counter-Ethics of Expediency." Cultural Studies and Critical Pedagogy Conference. The George Washington University, Washington, DC. 11 July 2006.

Hennessy, Rosemary. *Profit and Pleasure: Sexual Identities in Late Capitalism*. New York: Routledge, 2000.

Herndon, Sheri. "No Logo: A Conversation with Naomi Klein." *Indymedia.com*. 2000. <http://la.indymedia.org/news/2000/08/3496.php> 19 July 2006.

Hewett, Angela. "Whose Streets? Our Streets!" Conference of College Composition and Communication. Palmer House, Chicago. 26 March 2002.

Hewett, Angela, and Robert Mcruer. "Composing Student Activists: Relocating Student Writing. "*Public Works: Student Writing as Public Text*. Eds. Emily J. Isaacs & Phoebe Jackson. Portsmouth, NH: Boynton/Cook Heinemann Publishers, 2001: 97–108.

Jarratt, Susan. "Beside Ourselves: Rhetoric and Representation in Postcolonial Feminist Writing." *Journal of Advanced Composition*. 18:1 (1998): 57–75.

———. "Introduction: As We Were Saying . . ." *Feminism and Composition Studies: In Other Words*. New York: The Modern Language Association of America, 1998.

———. *Rereading the Sophists: Classical Rhetoric Refigured*. Carbondale: Southern Illinois University Press, 1991.

Kane, Anne. "Finding Emotion in Social Movement Processes: Irish Land Movement Metaphors and Narratives." *Passionate Politics: Emotions and Social Movements*. Eds.Jeff Goodwin, James Jaspar, and Francesca Polletta. Chicago: University of Chicago Press, 2001: 251– 266.

Kincaid, Jamaica. *Lucy*. New York: Farrar, Straus, Giroux, 1990.

———. *A Small Place*. New York: Farrar, Straus, Giroux, 2000.

Klein, Naomi. "Farewell to 'The End of History': Organization and Vision in Anti-Corporate Movements," *Socialist Register*. Eds. Leo Panitch and Colin Leys. London: Merlin Press, 2002: 1–14.

———. *No Logo*. New York: Picador, 1999.

Kristensen, Randi. "From *Things Fall Apart* to *Freedom Dreams*: Contact Zones in the Composition Classroom." Cultural Studies and Critical Pedagogy Conference. The George Washington University, Washington, DC. 10 July, 2006.

Kumar, Amitava. *World Bank Literature*. Minneapolis: University of Minnesota Press, 2003.

Lakoff, George. *Don't Think of an Elephant: Know Your Values and Frame the Debate*. White River Junction, VT: Chelsea Green, 2004.

Mahlis, Kristen. "Gender and Exile: Jamaica Kincaid's *Lucy*." *Modern Fiction Studies*. 44:1 (1998): 164–183.

Mahoney, Kevin. "The Diversion of Diversity." *AJAR*. 1.6 (1998): 3–4.

Marcos, Subcomandante. *Our Word Is Our Weapon*. Ed. Juana Ponce de Leon. New York· Seven Stories Press, 2001.

———.*Shadows of Tender Fury: The Letters and Communiques of Subcomandante Marcos and the Zapatista Army of National Liberation*. New York: Monthly Review Press, 1995.

Martin, Randy. "Artistic Citizenship." Cultural Studies Association. George Mason University, Fairfax, Virginia. 19 April 2006.

Marx, Karl. *The Eighteenth Brumaire of Louis Bonaparte*. New York: International Publishers, 1963.

———. *The German Ideology*. Ed. C.J. Arthur. New York: International Publishers, 1970.

McLaren, Peter, and Ramin Farahmandpur. "The Globalization of Capitalism and the New Imperialism: Notes Toward a Revolutionary Critical Pedagogy." *The Review of Education, Pedagogy, Cultural Studies.*, 23(2001): 271–315.

Mcruer, Robert. "As Good As It Gets: Queer Theory and Critical Disability." *GLQ*. 9:1–2 (2004): 79–105.

———. "Composing Bodies; or, De-Composition: Queer Theory, Disability Studies, and Alternative Corporealities." *Journal of Advanced Composition*. 24:1 (2004): 47–78.

———. *Crip Theory: Cultural Signs of Queerness and Disability*. New York: New York University Press, 2006.

———. Letter to Students. 16 April 2004.

Mies, Maria. *Patriarchy and Accumulation on a World Scale: Women in the International Division of Labour*. New York: Zed Books, 1998.

Miller, Carolyn. "Foreward." *Rhetoric and Kairos: Essays in History, Theory, and Praxis*. Eds. Phillip Sipiora and James S. Baumlin. Albany, NY: SUNY Press, 2002: 89–96.

Mohanty, Chandra. *Feminism Without Borders*. Durham, NC: Duke University Press, 2003.

Negri, Antonio. *Insurgencies: Constituent Power and the Modern State*. Trans. Maurizia Boscagli. Minneapolis: University of Minnesota Press, 1999.

Negt, Oskar, and Alexander Kluge. *Public Sphere and Experience: Toward an Analysis of the Bourgeois and Proletarian Public Sphere*. Trans. Peter Labanyi, et al. Minneapolis: University of Minnesota Press, 1993.

Nelson, Cary. "Literature as Cultural Studies: 'American' Poetry of the Spanish Civil War." *Disciplinarity and Dissent in Cultural Studies*. Eds. Cary Nelson and Dilip Parameshwar Gaonkar. New York: Routledge, 1996: 63–102.

Ngũgĩ wa Thiong'o. *Decolonizing the Mind: The Politics of Language in African Literature*. Portsmouth, NH: Heinemann, 1986.

Ohmann, Richard. *The Politics of Letters*. Middletown, CT: Wesleyan University Press, 1987.

Ong, Aiwha. *Spirits of Resistance and Capitalist Discipline: Factory Workers in Malaysia*. Albany, NY: State University of New York Press, 1987.

Plato. *Phaedrus. The Rhetorical Tradition: Readings from Classical Times to the Present*. Ed. Patricia Bizzell and Bruce Herzberg. Boston: Bedford/St. Martin's, 2001: 138–168.

Poulakos, John. "*Kairos* in Gorgias' Rhetorical Compositions." *Rhetoric and Kairos: Essays in History, Theory, and Praxis*. Ed. Phillip Sipiora and James S. Baumlin. Albany, NY: SUNY Press, 2002: 89–96.

Powell, Pegeen Reichert. "Critical Discourse Analysis and Composition Studies: A Study of Presidential Discourse and Campus Discord." *CCC*. 55:3 (2004): 439–69.

Rabasa, José. "Of Zapatismo: Reflections on the Folklorice and the Impossible in a Subaltern Insurrection." *The Latin American Subaltern Studies Reader*. Ed. Ileana Rodriguez. Durham, NC: Duke University Press, 2001: 561–583.

Riedner, Rachel. "Strategies of Containment." *Minnesota Review*. 61-62 (2004): 233–238.

Roy, Arundhati. "Confronting Empire." Z Net. Speech given at the World Social Forum in Porto Alegre, Brazil. 27 Jan 2003. <http://www.zmag.org/content/print_article.cfm?itemID=2919&section ID=51> 21 July 2006.

Ryder, Phyllis. "In(ter)ventions of Global Democracy: An Analysis of the Rhetorics of the A-16 World Bank/ IMF Protests in Washington, DC." *Rhetoric Review*. Forthcoming.

Smith, Holly. Personal Interview. 3 May 2004.

Smith, Neil. *The Endgame of Globalization*. New York: Routledge, 2005.

Sparr, Pamela. *Mortgaging Women's Lives: Feminist Critiques of Structural Adjustment*. Atlantic Highlands, NJ: Zed Books, 1994.

Spivak, Gayatri. *A Critique of Postcolonial Reason: Toward a History of the Vanishing Present*. Cambridge, MA: Harvard University Press, 1999.

———. *Death of a Discipline*. New York: Columbia University Press, 2003.

———. "Introduction." *Imaginary Maps: Three Stories*. Mahasweta Devi. Trans. by Gayatri Spivak. New York: Routledge, 1995.

———. "Righting Wrongs" *Human Rights, Human Wrongs: The Oxford Amnesty Lectures 2001*. Ed. Nicholas Owen. New York: Oxford University Press, 2003: 164–227.

———. "Scattered Speculations on the Question of Value." *In Other Worlds: Essays in Cultural Politics*. New York: Routledge, 1988.

———. "Thinking Cultural Questions in 'Pure' Literary Terms. *Without Guarantees: In Honour of Stuart Hall*. Eds. Paul Gilroy, Laurence Grossberg, Angela McRobbie. London and New York: Verso, 2000: 335–357.

Spurr, David. *The Rhetoric of Empire: Colonial Discourse in Journalism, Travel Writing, and Imperial Administration*. Durham, NC: Duke University Press, 1993.

Trimbur, John. *The Call to Write*. New York: Longman, 1999.

———."Composition and the Circulation of Writing." *CCC*. 52 (2000): 188–219.

Villanueva, Victor, Jr. *Bootstraps: From American Academic of Color*. Urbana, IL: NTCE, 1993.

Walkerdine, Valerie. "On the Regulation of Speaking and Silence" Subjectivity, Class, and Gender in Contemporary Schooling." *Language, Gender, and Childhood*. Ed. Carolyn Steedman, Cathy Urwin, and Valerie Walkerdine. London: Routledge and Kegan Paul, 1985: 203–241.

Warner, Michael. *Publics and Counterpublics*. New York: Zone Books, 2002.

Wells, Susan. "Rogue Cops and Health Care: What Do We Want from Public Writing?" *CCC*. 47:3 (1996): 325–341.

Williams, Raymond. *Communications*. London, Chatto & Windus, 1966.

———. *Keywords*. New York: Oxford University Press, 1976.

———. *Marxism and Literature*. Oxford: Oxford University Press, 1977.

Worsham, Lynn. "Coming to Terms: Theory, Writing, Politics." *Rhetoric and Composition as Intellectual Work*. Ed. Gary Olson. Carbondale: Southern Illinois University Press, 2002: 101–114.

Wright, Handel. "Dare We De-Centre Birmingham? Troubling the 'Origins' and Trajectories of Cultural Studies." *European Journal of Cultural Studies*. 1 (1998): 33–56.

Index

A-16 (April 16th, 2001), xiv, 1–6,
  8, 13, 40, 91
A Small Place, 53–55
academic institution, *See* university
academic rhetoricians, *See* cultural
  studies
Adorno, Theodore, xv–xvi
affect, xv; affective experience, 6;
  24; and hegemony, 47; as
  rhetorical action, 64, 66–67, 81,
  99; as excess of hegemony, 78
Ahmed, Sara, 7, 47, 51
Angus, Ian, 79–80
Aristotle, x, 25
Augustine, ix–x, xii

Bakhtin M.M., 10; language, 99
benevolence, xv, 52–67; and neoliberalism, 55; as rhetoric, 55;
  and gendered labor, 59–61; and
  value, 58–59; citizen consumer,
  61; 71
Birmingham School, 9
Bourdieu, Pierre, xvi; and strong
  rhetoric 10, 13n3; 20, 41;
  on habitus, 75, 77
Brown, Danika, 27
Butler, Judith, xiv, xvi, 1, 5, 6, 24;
  on performativity, 50n1, 88,
  89, 90; and rhetorical action,
  103

Chang, Grace, 60–62
Cicero, ix
Cleaver, Harry, 26–27
composition, 9–10, 92
conjunctural, as cultural studies
  term, xiv and 8; neoliberalism,
  17–18, 43–44; conjunctural
  moment, 88, *See also* Gramsci
counter-public, and public sphere,
  x–xi
critical pedagogy, *See* pedagogy
critical thinking, 107n22
cultural studies, xii, 9–10; and
  pedagogy, 13n1; and academic
  rhetoric, 89–95; and literacy,
  102

de Man, Paul, 24
democracy, and pedagogy, xiii–xiv;
  in neoliberal world, 5; as
  rhetoric, 88
democracy-to-come, xiv, 9, 94–95,
  104, 105n2
Derrida, Jacques, 11, 19, 24; and
  rhetoric, 25, 89; and difference, 91
despair, and hopelessness, xv; and
  neoliberalism, 70–71, 75–76,
  80–82; and democracy, 71; and
  left discourse, 73
différance, 19, 63, 103

Ellsworth, Elizabeth, 73, 77
Emma Goldman, 2
emotion, and rhetorical action, xv;
    as political work and activism,
    8; as pedagogy, 9; and value,
    39, 46; as cultural politics, 52;
    as value, 56; social move-
    ment, 81; as irrational, 81; and
    collective power, 83–84; and
    habitus, 84. *See also* structures of
    feeling
empire. *See* neoliberalism
Empire. See Hardt and Negri

Ferguson, Roderick, 63–64, 67n2
Foucault, Michael, 89
Fraser, Nancy, 12, 35
Freire, Paolo, 5, 6, 9, 10, 33; on
    integration, 36n3, 69; and
    hope, 82, 84. *See also* pedagogy
Fukuyama, Francis, 35, 69–71; and
    neoliberalism, 70; and despair,
    70–71, 79

George, Diana, 7, 61
George Washington University, 36,
    42–49, 53–55
Giroux, Henry, 20–21, 32
Gorgias, xi, 23
Gramsci, Antonio, 9, 10, 23; rheto-
    ric, 30–31, 43–44; and hege-
    mony, 47–48; and consent, 48;
    common sense, 81

Habermas, Juergen, xi, 86n3
Hall, Stuart, xiv, and ideology, 57–
    58; 89
Hardt, Michael and Antonio Negi,
    6, 7, 10, 12, 13, 22, 36n4, 49;
    and emotion, 63, 84; and
    society of control, 80, 89;
    and radical political move-
    ments, 93–94; and affect, 102–
    107n23
Harvey, David, 11; and neoliberal-
    ism, 19, 22–23, 35
Hewett, Angela, 5, 25

Hipp, Jason, 34

Imaginary Maps, 64
International Monetary Fund (IMF),
    and protests, xiii, 1, 3, 65. *See also*
    A-16
Irish Land Movement, 82-84

Jarratt, Susan, 8, 18, 19, 20, 25, 67;
    on Plato 81, 90

kairos, x, xiii, 23–24; and Zapatista
    writing, 23, 91; and rhetorical
    action, 104, 105n7
Keywords, See Raymond Williams
Kincaid, Jamaica. *See A Small
    Place* and *Lucy*
Klein, Naomi, 72
Kumar, Amitava, 40, 53

labor, and democracy, 18; as a so-
    cial relation, 27; and univer-
    sity, 46; and benevolence, 53,
    60–61
Lakoff, George, 73–74
Literacy. *See* pedagogy
Lucy, 64–66

Marcos, Subcomandante, 1, 11, 24,
    87–88, 90, 105n12
Marx, Karl, 22; failure of class, 61-
    62; and radical political move-
    ments, 93–94
Mcruer, Robert, 21, 25, 27, 36
Mohanty, Chandra, 4, 11

Negt, Oskar and Alexander Kluge,
    25–26, 35; and bourgeois pub-
    lic sphere, 85
neoliberalism, and public sphere,
    xi; as pedagogy, xiii; as writ-
    ing, 10–11, 39–40; and emotion,
    xv, 39–49; and writing, 11; as
    public pedagogy, 18–27, 46–49,
    51, 88; as rhetoric, 10, 19–20,
    25, 39, 88; as persuasion, 39–
    40; and hegemony, 77–79; and

despair, 80–81; and university, 102–103

pedagogy, as cultural and political, xi, xiii; and democracy-to-come, xiv; as cultural literacy, xiv; and university, xiv; as praxis of learning, 3; and democracy, 7, 89, 105n2; and institutions, 8; of freedom, 8; for liberation, 9; and affect, 11; as social practice, 11; as practice, 12; as cultural and political intervention; and rhetorical action, 88; as kairotic and teleopoetic, 104
persuasion, ix–xi
Plato, 74; on rationality and emotion, 81
pre-emergent, xv
production, xi. *See also* labor
Progressive Student Union, 42–43
Poulakos, John, 23–25
Powell, Pegeen Reikhart, 11–12
public sphere, and counter-public sphere, x–xi, 86

radical cheerleaders, 2
rhetoric, 9; and emotion, 22; and democracy, 24
rhetorical action, xi, xiv, 7, 8, 17; for political struggle, 24–25, 29–33; and emotion and affect, 41; and new literacies, 50n3; and affect, 64, 66, 72, 74, 88–89; and excess, 88; and affective action, 99; and academic work, 101; and gender, 103–104
Roman Empire, ix
Roy, Arundhati, xvi, 69
Ryder, Phyllis, 2–3, 6

shame, 84
Spivak, Gayatri, xvi; on pedagogy, 7; 11; on value, 19–20; and benevolence, 53, 56–58; and ethics, 62; on difference, 62,

64–66, 89, 90; and academic rhetoric, 107n24
structures of feeling, xi, 23–24, 27, 36, 39–41, 43, 50–52; and neoliberalism, 71, 99. *See also* Raymond Williams
surplus value, 62–64

teaching, 13, 30, 32; and neoliberalism, 46
teaching of writing, 1–2, 6, 11, 34, 54–55, 67n4, 71–86
teleopoeisis, 90–91; and rhetorical action, 104
Thatcher, Margaret, 70, 72
"The Story of the Tiny Cat and the Tiny Mouse," 96–101
Trimbur, John, 92, 106n15

university, and pedagogy, xiv, 12, neoliberalism and labor, 17–18; as social relation, 29, 67

value, 37n2; and emotion, 39–40, 56–59

Wells, Susan, 11
Williams, Raymond, 1, 8, 11, 21–22, 24, 27; on education, 32–34; on hegemony, 48, 74; on structures of feeling, 23–24, 27, 36, 39–41, 43, 50–52; 77; and emotion, 62, 75, 89
World Bank, and protests, xiii, 2, 3, 65. *See also* A-16
World Trade Organization, 74

Zapatistas, xv; and neoliberalism, 21; and writing, 24, and openness to democracy, 24, 36, 49; and rhetoric 88–90, 91–93, 95–100; and rhetorical action, 102; and time, 105n8; and laughter, 98–99, 106n17, 107n19

About the Authors

Rachel Riedner is Assistant Professor of University Writing at The George Washington University. She has essays published in *Enculturation, the minnesota review,* and the *Journal of Advanced Composition. Democracies to Come* is her first book.

Kevin Mahoney is an Associate Professor of Composition at Kutztown University of Pennsylvania. In addition to his academic work, he is an activist and local leader in his union, APSCUF. His research and teaching interests include literacy and globalization, radical pedagogy, rhetoric and democracy, rhetoric of advocacy, autonomous education and social movements. *Democracies to Come* is his first book.